"*Three Months: A Caregiving Journey from Heartbreak to Healing* is the heart-wrenching and heart-warming account of the challenges, changes, and courage a couple faces when one is diagnosed with terminal cancer. This book is a tribute to both spouses—Margaret's strength and grace in the final months of her life as well as the story of Diet's determination and love as he takes on a new role, that of caregiver. The guidance and resources referenced in this book can help those who find themselves serving as a health advocate and navigating a range of complex decisions and emotions. *Three Months* is a rare combination—a love story and a handbook—that will speak to anyone who has been or who will be responsible for the care of a loved one."

—*Dr. Thomas Peters, President & CEO, Marin Community Foundation and former Director of Health, Marin County*

"*Three Months: A Caregiving Journey from Heartbreak to Healing* is a most poignant and passionate account of the discovery of a successful path for one very loving spouse to survive the inevitable death of the other spouse facing terminal cancer. The lessons *Three Months* teaches are practical, pragmatic, caring and even redemptive. *Three Months: A Caregiving Journey from Heartbreak to Healing*, miraculously, makes both life and death seem better."

—*Gary T. Giacomini, Former Marin County Supervisor and Cancer Survivor*

Published 2012
ISBN: 978-0-9822888-5-6

Book design by Focus Design
www.focusd.com

Folkheart Press
PO Box 241
Cotati, CA 94928
www.folkheartpress.com

Printed in the United States of America

Three Months

A Caregiving Journey from Heartbreak to Healing

by J. Dietrich Stroeh & Bill Meagher

To Laura
A short time
in life

Diet

To have
A short time
in fit
Dick

Dedication

Margaret,
a beautiful and compassionate
woman.

Foreword

Life is mysterious. Its cycles are powerful. At times efforts to understand them drive some to go beyond what their society tells them to be true. Namely that being alive is all about what happens before death; that dying itself is not part of life's rhythms. Not so according to *Three Months: A Caregiving Journey from Heartbreak to Healing*. In this moving book which chronicles the abrupt loss of a loved one to pancreatic cancer, J. Dietrich Stroeh embarks upon a quest that is known in folklore as the Hero's Journey.

Sharing as he does in this manuscript the personal nature of a universal truth that all living things die, Diet travels to and then beyond the edges of mortality. Initially, this unexpectedly finds him powerless. Unable to call upon his own strengths to alter the course of life's final mystery, he has to overcome internal weaknesses and external obstacles so he can do what he must do: take care of his wife and, when the time comes, lovingly let her go. He has to come to terms with her end of life so he can continue to live.

Everyday beliefs about life passages can be expressed in a variety of ways, including writing. *Three Months: A Caregiving Journey from Heartbreak to Healing* recounts what Diet has learned the hard way in the hopes that these lessons will benefit others.

It is an honor to publish such a book,

Karen
Karen Pierce Gonzalez
Publisher, Folkheart Press
http://www/folkheartpress.com

Preface

"It is strange how a heart must be broken before the years can make it wise." —American Poet Sara Teasdale

It's like getting hit in the head with a hammer.

There's simply no way to prepare yourself for the moment when you are seated across that neatly organized desk from a doctor, a doctor who may or may not make eye contact when he says the words that change things irrevocably in ways you can't even name.

You wake up one morning and the day moves along at its own pace; things make sense. Then your doctor picks up a folder and begins to speak.

Your world has a new shape and all of yesterday's problems and challenges are grainy and gray. He says the word "cancer". Now you know where your soul is because a stream of fear and anger and sadness spill out of it.

I consider myself an intelligent man. I have spent my life as an engineer working on things that require measurement. My days are filled with solving problems and seeing projects taking shape from bare land. You want something done, give it to me and I will figure out how to make it happen. It's what I am good at.

Maybe I was naive. When the doctor said "pancreatic cancer," I was thinking I could do this, I could do that. But then it begins to sink in. It's almost like you are stupid. You sit there as if there might be a deal to be made. In my head I was saying, "I'll do whatever they tell me to do."

For a moment there must have been calm and I looked around for a way to bargain.

But that moment passes and too soon your life is no longer about what is easy or maybe what's possible. It's no longer smooth edges or level playing fields or a horizon that is easily seen.

There is nothing easy about hearing a doctor say your wife has pancreatic cancer. But as hard as that moment is, what comes after is so much harder. And it's the reason I wrote this book.

The thing about life is this. At some point, everyone sits in that office and everyone has that horrible moment. You might be alone with the doctor, or you may be with loved ones. But that room will be quiet and the air will be still and the doctor will tell you that your wife or father or child, or you, have a disease and that disease is likely to send you away for good. At the very least, he will tell you that you are in for the fight of your life and the stakes are like nothing you have ever considered.

And in those few seconds, everything changes. Maybe you will wish you were smarter, or had better luck, or maybe even that it was you that had that disease, that somebody else could be spared what is to come. If you are a man, you may wish for strength, to somehow hold your emotions in check even as your heart fills with such anguish you're sure it will stop.

Then there is the fear because so much of what's coming is a scary mystery. More than the unexplored territory is the reality that so much is riding on these decisions, decisions that will mean everything.

Some people may leap into making bargains with their God, offering to live differently if only the terrible circumstances can be altered.

For my part, I can't tell you what to do about that moment, despite the fact I have lived it over and over since it happened. In some ways it's hard not to live it over.

But what I can do is tell you what to expect in those moments after that pronouncement, when the earth begins to spin again. The sad truth is while it feels as if someone has yanked air from the room and there is a dull white noise buzzing in your head, the world will not be slowed by any bargain you make. And though people have a phenomenal ability to help you, in the end you need to find a way to function despite your life, or that of a loved one, being shattered.

While this story is about heartbreak and anguish, it is also a tale of survival and redemption. This book will give you common sense tools to help you deal with hours of waiting for news that you may not want. We will talk about how to navigate the maze that is modern healthcare, about how to be an advocate for your own health or that of a loved one. We will also look at the hurdles of everyday life that will continue despite the fact that your life may never look or feel the same. In short we will tell you how to not only endure, but how to find your hope. The alternate chapters will tell the story of my wife Margaret's struggle and how we spent our last three months together. Every other chapter will focus on a piece of the caregiver's experience, real life examples and resources that will help you know what to expect and how to find your own way through this journey.

Along the way, you will meet Margaret, a beautiful woman and the center of my life. You will feel the warmth of our home and smell homemade apple pie. You will hear her laughter and see oak trees dotting our hills, as well as the vegetables we raised in her garden. You will know Margaret's joy and you will feel her life slipping away slowly, and then very quickly.

You will walk the streets of Reno and take a plane to Dallas. You will meet our children and sit in a sick room as cancer blots out the light.

Ernest Hemmingway once wrote *"all true stories end in death"*. This is a true story.

Table of Contents

Chapter 1

Margaret and Me

*"I'm so optimistic I'd go after Moby Dick in a row boat and
take the tartar sauce with me."* —*Zig Ziglar*

Like a lot of busy people, Margaret and I met in the office, the place
where both of us spent a lot of time. This was long before online match-
making or even personal ads in the newspaper.

At the time I was the General Manager of the Marin Municipal
Water District, the agency responsible for supplying water to most of
Marin County, an affluent part of the San Francisco Bay Area. As luck
would have it, I was in charge of the district during the worst drought
in the county's history. It required us to not only think outside the box,
but to blow the box up and rebuild it to make sure Marin had enough
water. It made for some very long days and longer nights spent at public meetings. Meeting the public in Marin can be an experience testing
your patience. The combination of a population with a high degree of
education, affluence, free time and entitlement means the public process
explores many different directions, some of them productive, and some
of them a complete waste of time.

Most people find change a challenge, and the people who live between the Golden Gate Bridge and the Wine Country are no exception.

Telling people they need to change the way they use an everyday thing like water was harder than it is now, as the world has adopted a broader view of the importance of the environment. Talking to people about taking shorter showers, not washing their cars and planting drought resistant gardens in a place where million-dollar homes were more the norm than the exception wasn't easy.

Margaret was my administrative assistant at the District, a job requiring her to be completely organized herself, and to also keep me on track, not a small job by itself. It wasn't easy given the fact that we were involved in projects like building a pipeline across the Richmond-San Rafael Bridge to bring water to Marin. She made my job easier, acting as a good-natured gatekeeper, allowing me to get my work done in part by limiting access of others to my office. She was subtly protective of me even then. She didn't care much for the politics that went along with providing water for Marin or for the age-old tug of war between development interests and no-growth backers, but she understood the process and knew who the players were. While I always found her friendly and easy to talk to, our relationship was always strictly professional.

But one night, after a public meeting that included plenty of the public participation Marin is well known for, I was more than ready for a drink and some quiet. Margaret and I decided to get a drink together. We spent a lot of time that evening talking about the office and the meeting. At the end of the evening, we were in my car and we found ourselves kissing, despite the fact that neither of us had ever expressed any feelings for the other. That night signaled a change in my life.

I was intrigued and excited and to a degree, confused. I was married and that relationship had been changing. Although Margaret didn't make a habit of sharing her feelings about her marriage with me, I knew that in the past she and her husband had been through some rough spots.

I thought if Margaret and I talked about it a bit it might help so I suggested a drive to one of the District's reservoirs and she said yes. Off we went to Tomales Bay talking and driving. At one point I felt as if I was in high school, alone with a beautiful girl in my car, but not for long.

2

I reached over to kiss her, but she stopped me, "No, no, I really need to think this through," she said.

Margaret was heading back East to see her family for a week and I knew this would give her time to think as well as putting some distance between us. I wasn't looking forward to her leaving but I knew it would help her gain some perspective on us, whatever we were.

While I wanted her to find comfort and understand our situation better, that didn't mean I wanted to have her forget about me or that I wanted to stop talking to her. While she was gone, I called her at her sister's a couple of times and we talked.

When she returned, we began eating lunch together; going over to Scoma's when it was at Larkspur Landing or maybe Chalet Basque out past the Civic Center. Something was starting to grow between us. The more time we spent talking, the more comfortable we were with each other and the closer we seemed to become.

Over the next year and a half, our relationship took shape. An ease grew between us and our bond formed, first of friendship and then with time, something else. One day she came out with it and said her marriage was falling apart. She was having difficulties in her family and finally decided she was moving out. Her divorce came quickly after that. We began spending more time out of the office together, eating dinner and talking.

In the meantime, it was becoming plain to me that my marriage wasn't going to go the distance.

Complicating the situation for me was the fact that I had three teenage daughters. Christine was the oldest at 17, Jody was 15 and Erica was just 13. While I knew that the relationship with my wife was to say the least a little confusing, I could only imagine how my girls were trying to make sense of it. The time came when I knew what made sense for me and my family was for me to move out and find my own place and my own way.

My wife and I tried to do the best we could with the kids and with each other as we headed toward divorce. Our family had dinner one night and we divided up the assets and liabilities. It was very civilized which made a difficult time a little easier for the whole family.

By this time Margaret had bought a home in Petaluma and I was spending weekends with her. We were spending more time together, becoming more important in each other's lives.

In 1985 Margaret and I were ready for the next step. We wanted to get married. As it turns out it wasn't that simple. On Good Friday, we went to the Civic Center to get a license and as the clerk was filling out the paperwork she looked up and stopped as a strange look crossed her face. "You can't get married," she said. I was staring at her and asked why not? "She said, "Because you are still married."

I was dumbfounded but Margaret's mouth was working fine, "What the hell are you doing?" she asked, her voice leaving little doubt that she was unhappy. I explained to the clerk and to Margaret that my divorce papers had recently been completed and turned in. Was there any chance, I asked, that they were waiting someplace in the office to be processed?

The clerk did some checking and sure enough she found them in a stack of papers waiting to be entered into the system. We didn't get married that day but now we had a good story to tell.

After all the paperwork made it to the right place, we were married at a good friend's home and later honeymooned in Monterey, a place both of us loved.

We started our lives together. Though both of us were far from being kids, I felt a little like a youngster, with a renewed energy and a sense that our lives were full of possibility and opportunities. No matter where things took us, we would make our way happily.

Chapter 2

What Now?

"Life is like an ice cream cone, you have to learn to lick it!"
— Charlie Brown of "Peanuts" fame

The hardest part about having your world come apart at the seams is that the rest of the world doesn't miss a beat. Rudyard Kipling started his epic poem "If" with these words: "If you can keep your head when all about you are losing theirs…" I might finish that sentence with these words: "then you just haven't had a chance to think things all the way through."

That is where these alternating chapters come in. Every other chapter, I will focus on one aspect of care giving. My experience taking care of Margaret was full of helpful advice, trial and error, best guesses and dumb luck. I will do my best to share all of that in the hope that it will make your journey easier.

One thing I learned in caring for Margaret was there was an almost constant search for balance inside my head between my emotions and logic. Emotionally I was devastated by the seriousness of her illness, how it impacted her health and how it made me feel. At the same time, I knew I needed to keep my emotions in check not only so I could care for Margaret effectively, but also so she would not take any emotional cues from me that could make her feel worse.

And no matter what your brain tells you about a treatment or a conversation with a doctor, there is always an emotional response as well, one that is not always easy to quell or set aside. We will talk more about the balance between reason and emotion later. For now, let's focus on reason.

For the purpose of these chapters, let's assume you are caring for a loved one who faces a life threatening illness. This means you're learning on the fly and may need to make quick decisions. Putting a game plan together that will allow you to do this requires adopting a fundamental tenet of modern living: information is power.

This goes beyond understanding where the information is, but also who can supply it and explain what that information means to you and your family. In an amazingly short period of time, you will face specialists, doctors, nurses, administrators, social workers and aides, and they will all be fluent in a language you have only heard on TV when one of the doctors on ER shouted to hang another bag of AB negative, stat! Sitting at home you don't need to know the difference between AB negative and A&W Root Beer. But with a loved one lying in intensive care, understanding what members of the medical team are telling you is critical.

No matter how simple or complicated the medical challenge is, when the doctor discusses it with you, you should take notes and ask questions regarding anything you don't understand. Do it right then, while you are confused, not later when you might not recall the subject. On the surface, this may seem simplistic, but having an accurate record of what needs to happen will help you understand what does, or doesn't come next.

The point here is to advocate on behalf of your loved one. While your doctor is learned and has impressive diplomas hanging in the office and a three week waiting list for an appointment, this does not preclude you from asking him or her questions. Indeed, understanding all you can not only about the illness, but the treatment options, will make you feel as if you are making a difference in the treatment. And believe me, you will come to understand that there is quite a bit that will happen that you can't control. Understanding what you can change and why is key.

In the past we were conditioned to put medical professionals on a pedestal and to treat doctors as if they were royalty, or at the very least non-reality TV stars. But many studies conducted in recent years have revealed a startling fact; doctors and nurses are human! And while they are capable of healing at a level that can be hard to fathom, likewise they can make mistakes like everyone else.

Medical professionals have begun to understand that their patients and their caregivers have a right to accurate information. Patient's privacy rights can make this information exchange complicated. There are now federal and state privacy laws that give patients specific rights to privacy where medical data is concerned. So either forging an understanding with your doctor or filing the proper legal forms is critical to keeping the information flowing.

While patients and their caregivers need accurate information, the distribution of information in a timely fashion needs to be balanced by understanding your doctors and nurses have other patients as well. While the care your loved one is receiving is the focus of your world, realistically it is a slice of the world in which your doctor and other medical personal live. Keeping that in perspective will help you build an effective line of communication and relationship with those who will be providing care.

Now, let's dip into the emotional side. Given that the vast majority of us are not doctors, the simple pronouncement of a disease and its likely outcome by a physician will launch a series of fears that can dominate our thinking and pierce our core until simple movement and communication seem almost beyond hope. The biggest fear of all is that the disease will take the life of our loved one. But there are a variety of fears related to this one that can slow you down as well. Most of us desire a fair amount of control over our lives, but a life-threatening illness can leave you feeling as if that control is being taken away. Related to this is a fear of becoming a burden on those we love should we need help caring for ourselves. We fear the economic repercussions should the illness begin draining our financial resources. We fear everything from the perceived change in social status that long-term illness can bring to the loss of important relationships in our lives. So acknowledging the fears and taking steps to lessen their impacts is fundamental to functioning as well as caring for others. Accessing and understanding information is a very effective way to battle these fears.

Another emotional reality is that the stress of caring for a loved one fighting for their life may leave you a little short in the emotional well-being department. Keeping that in mind as you interact with hospital staff can go a long way towards getting the information and the treatment that will most benefit your loved one.

From the most exalted specialists doing surgery to the people in the kitchen putting cellophane on the Jell-O, they are all your new medical teammates. Treating everyone at the hospital, clinic or doctor's office with respect and kindness matters a great deal, no matter what the pain or prognosis. Modern medicine on its best day is a complicated over-the-top expensive maze of hoops, hurdles and regulations that can seem almost impossible to navigate.

You're going to need a lot of help to traverse this difficult territory. And while the illness may require an intricate operation, you will be shocked at what a shift nurse can accomplish on your behalf if you treat them with the same dignity and respect you hope to receive. Not to preach, but the Golden Rule can do much good when dealing with folks who wear scrubs.

Chapter 3

"I Feel Full"

There is a time when spring is not quite gone and summer hasn't taken its full measure in our neighborhood. The hills still have flowers in bloom and the grasses that carpet the slopes are green. The days almost grudgingly grow longer and the deer on our property linger, worrying less about their safety and more about whether that bush over there is delicious or not.

One of our summertime pursuits was spending time by the pool. Margaret and I would take to the pool to relax and cool off. When summer comes to Marin, the mercury creeps into the 70's and 80's, the kind of heat that is easy to work in and makes you appreciate the beauty that surrounds you.

While our summer routines included working the garden as well as time by the pool, we also found time for trips both great and small. As spring gave way to summer, we went to Nevada for one of my alumni functions at the University of Reno, staying for a couple of days at Circus Circus. In July we got away for a weekend in Santa Cruz. When we got home, I thought Margaret looked a bit tired, but thought nothing more about it. She also began saying that at times she felt full, but neither of us thought there was anything wrong.

Fall came to Marin as the trees changed color and dropped their leaves. One of the things we liked to do when summer faded away was to spend some time with our two apple trees, harvesting the sweet Gravenstein apples for pies and canning. It's a tradition that got started simply and grew over 20 years. Margaret decided to try her hand at baking and I had grown up helping my mom do pies, sometimes sitting for hours at a stretch, peeling the ripe fruit. Though there is no official standing on this, I might be the world's greatest apple peeler.

Margaret and I put a process together. We started with store bought pie crusts and used a little lemon water to keep the apples from turning color. Margaret created a paste of almonds, walnuts, and pecans mixed with butter cinnamon, nutmeg and vanilla. I became her sous chef, chopping the nuts. We would put the apples in the crust, then top the fruit with maybe half an inch of the paste and then bake for 35 minutes. We would freeze the pies and pull them out of the freezer all year to enjoy. We might make 15 or 20 pies with our little assembly line. We also discovered they make great gifts as they are delicious, homemade and personal. Our friends and family grew to enjoy our pies and looked forward to the winter when our "pie shop" would be up and running.

Baking the pies wasn't about having dessert or stocking the freezer; it was about us being together. While we worked, we talked about everything, catching up on each other's lives, sharing stories and laughing. Talking was always easy for us, but so was silence. Neither of us felt the pressure to fill it in; we could simply be together and enjoy it.

With the pies, we fell into a routine that felt right. I was the apple peeler, using the same peeler I had used for my mom's pies. The gadget was old and worn, but felt right in my hands. It was perfect because Margaret didn't like peeling. But one day she surprised me with a new peeler. It was sparkling and high tech and I wanted no part of it. She thought I was nuts, but the old peeler was the right tool for the job.

We liked to take drives together, not really with any special plan or errands to run. We would simply get in the car and hit the road for a few hours. I'd suggest we take a ride and she would leave it to me to pick the place. We would find a place along the way to have a bite to eat. Sometimes we drove out to Tomales and did something as simple as watching the Red Tail Hawks soar in the wind coming off the bay. There was a joy we shared in simply observing these beautiful birds.

While I was the driver, Margaret led in other ways. She was the keeper of our culture. We liked going to the American Conservatory Theater in San Francisco, making a night of it with dinner before the show. She was plugged into what was going on at the museums, always knowing if a new exhibit was in town.

Both of us enjoyed the movies, both traditional first run films and independent movies. We helped with the restoration of the Rafael Theater in San Rafael and frequently saw movies there. We took informal turns picking out movies. We loved the classics. We would see a movie and then come out and become critics. I learned to let Margaret lead the way before I said anything. If she said, "What did you think," that was code for "I'm not sure I liked that one."

Another way we fit together was that I am an optimist and she tended to see the glass as half empty. Lots of married couples are opposites in some way and I guess we were no exception. Like others, we found our rhythms, the way that felt right and in some ways it was a subtle guide for us. I was always the one who saw lots of different possibilities in things and Margaret kept me in check by playing the devil's advocate, showing me the other side of the situation, taking it apart so that I saw something that wasn't there before.

We made a very good team.

While I was at the office, Margaret would sometimes go to the Margaret Todd Center in Novato and work out or have lunch with friends. She also became an expert at bridge, often playing with friends at the Center.

She exercised every day, walking much more than I did. She never smoked and drank very little. She really was the picture of health and she would get after me about wearing a hat in the sun or forgetting sunscreen. "Diet, where are your sunglasses?" she would ask with a tone that let me know that she loved me, and that I had better find my glasses.

There are people who can't look at a houseplant without inflicting harm while others seem to naturally relate to things that grow. Margaret always had a green thumb and she loved working in our garden, raising plenty of the vegetables we ate. One of our routines as the seasons changed was to spend more time working in the garden. At the time I didn't honestly realize something was changing, but nonetheless a subtle shift was at work. Margaret still worked the garden and still did the little things, but now it was she who would say, "OK, let's quit for the day." And I was the one who said there was more to be done.

The change was there in other ways too, but still so subtle. I wanted to put in some new flowers and I asked her what she thought of the new additions. She always loved her flowers but now she didn't have much of an opinion on how the new choices might look in the garden. She also said that we were growing too many vegetables, and "too many vegetables" was not Margaret. She always ate the right food—healthy whole grains, salmon or other fish and very little red meat.

Her cooking became a little erratic. It wasn't that our meals were bad. The food was still delicious, but sometimes a dish was under or over cooked, and this was unusual because she was a helluva cook. There were times when I wasn't quite sure what we were eating, some kind of lentils perhaps or an exotic rice or grain. I never asked, learning long ago not to question the one who feeds you. Besides, it was delicious.

As Thanksgiving approached, we prepared for our annual trip to Texas, to have the holiday at our house in the Lone Star State. We also visited with Margaret's family, including her mother who turned 90 the weekend following Turkey Day.

The flight down was uneventful, with both of us reading books and dozing a little. We followed a tradition of many years, traveling to New Braunfels to the Menger Hotel that does an amazing Thanksgiving buffet. While they have turkey and all the trimmings, they also serve ham, venison, roast beef and even some Tex-Mex dishes. The desserts are unbelievable. Everybody was dressed up and we had a great time.

While everyone tends to eat too much at Thanksgiving, Margaret was not among them. Don't get me wrong, she enjoyed herself, but while the rest of us were stuffing ourselves, Margaret was not feasting at the same rate. So when she remarked that she felt full, it was different than any of the rest of us.

To honor her mom, Margaret and her family organized a 90th birthday party. It was held at her mom's retirement home and about 150 people were there. Margaret, who went through life as a bit of a camp counselor, was anxious about the party, wanting to be sure it was what her mom wanted and that everyone would come and have a good time. Though Margaret was not one for the spotlight or giving speeches, she was planning on saying something. I knew she was nervous about doing it and offered to stand in for her. "No, no, I'll do it," she said, her voice showing a little of the nerves. When the time came, I spoke up and asked for everyone's attention. With her brother and sister standing next to her, she welcomed everyone with something off the top of her head that really was quite nice. She praised her mom and while the speech wasn't going to remind anyone of Honest Abe, it was warm and fuzzy and felt good. She did a helluva job.

When we got back to the house early that evening, she looked tired and went to bed early while the rest of us stayed up and visited.

We flew home on Sunday out of the San Antonio Airport. The flight was scheduled for just one stop and we settled into our seats. As Margaret made herself at home, she groaned a little and I asked her if she was OK. "I feel full, stuffed."

"You are probably feeling the effects of Thanksgiving," I said.

She shook her head and disagreed.

We both cracked open our books and read for awhile. After a bit, Margaret fell asleep. I watched her for awhile and was struck by the lines around her eyes, which made her look tired. In hindsight, perhaps they were lines caused by pain, but at the time I did not make the connection.

She woke up after nodding off for a bit and we talked about the trip. She was happy that the party for her mom had gone so well and seeing her family also made her feel good. What didn't make her happy was her stomach. Again, she complained about feeling full and I suggested that when we got home she should make an appointment with her primary doctor, Dr. Schmidt. The rest of the flight was uneventful, which is nice when you are on an airplane. Boring is good in mid-air. We both were in our own thoughts. I was worried about Margaret and her fullness, but I didn't say anything about it. I honestly thought it was simply a minor stomach problem.

We got home late Sunday night and didn't bother to unpack and Margaret went right to bed. The next day, she called Dr. Schmidt for an appointment. She couldn't get in to see her until later in the week. Margaret spent the rest of the week feeling stuffed as she became more and more bloated.

When she did see her doctor, the initial exam didn't give us anything to work with so Dr. Schmidt scheduled a sonogram for the following week. She said without more tests she couldn't nail down what was bothering Margaret.

We waited another week. If Margaret's feeling full was becoming a pattern, so was the waiting. Modern medicine has given us a cure for many things and has helped us in many amazing ways. Yet there is still no cure for how slowly the clock on the wall moves when someone is in pain, nor a cure for how long the days are when you are waiting for an answer or for how fleeting the weeks are when someone you love is dying.

All the time we spent looking at the calendar, my Margaret spent hurting. She could no longer sleep lying down, rather, she had to prop herself up with two or three pillows. Even then, her sleep came in fits and starts.

Finally, the day came for her sonogram. I know we were both looking forward to the exam to get some answers as well as getting Margaret to a place where she would feel normal. But the initial exam was inconclusive, showing nothing that would cause her the discomfort that had become her daily nemesis.

Later that night, upon reviewing the test results further, they found water in the abdominal cavity. The doctors wanted to drain the fluid, a procedure known as puncturing the peritoneal cavity.

Again, it took days to set up the procedure, and in the meantime Margaret suffered. When she did have the procedure, she felt better, but we still had no idea how or why the fluid was in her stomach.

So the doctors requested a CAT scan. The good news about this test was we could go to the emergency room and have the work done right away.

The bad news about this test was we found out what the problem was, and that news broke my heart.

Chapter 4

Be Your Own GPS:
Navigate the Medical Maze

"Asking is the beginning of receiving.
Make sure you don't go to the ocean with a teaspoon. At least take
a bucket so the kids don't laugh at you." —Jim Rohn

One of the most maddening things about caring for a loved one is the medical maze. And here, I am not talking about the elaborate labyrinth known as medical insurance, HMO's or even PPO's. No, I refer to the obstacle course that is laid out before millions of patients and caregivers each day at a time when the last thing they need is one more hurdle.

It begins with how we communicate with our doctors, moves on to how appointments are scheduled and at times becomes even more frustrating when you end up seeing a doctor.

Our everyday world is chock full of paths for communication. The Blackberry/Droid phone/iPhone/Intergalatic communication device has become so commonplace that pay phones are only seen in Superman movies. We email with abandon, video with ease, text till our thumbs are on fire and Twitter to our hearts content at 140 words a slug. We MySpace, Facebook, Skype and blog about everything and nothing at all.

But for the most part, our communications with the people we trust with our health still begins at the other end of the telephone, the same way they did 50 years ago. And despite all of the technology that will fit in our pockets and on our desks, it isn't likely to change much.

We request an appointment with our doctor because something isn't right, and we hope there is an opening that will fit with our increasingly busy lives, or failing that, will cause the least amount of disruption. We go from focusing on our health to focusing on how we can somehow fit our health concerns into our day.

So this is our starting point: The accepted model is for you the patient, to call your trusted medical pro and beg for a slice of time. But what about a new idea on how we approach the relationship we or our loved ones have with our physicians? What if we instead viewed ourselves as clients and the doctor as the consultant we employ? Would that change the dynamic at all?

Maybe.

I'm not talking about a revolution in the relationship between doctor and patient. I am calling for a change as a first step towards patients becoming effective advocates for themselves and advocates becoming more effective as well.

My parent's generation grew up idolizing doctors and viewed those in medicine as royalty. Doctors granted you an audience and if you were lucky enough to see them, any diagnosis or advice was understood to be akin to carved on a stone tablet. A second opinion was something handed down from an appeals court. When the doctor prescribed a drug to cure what ailed you, there wasn't a discussion of drug interaction or side-effects. Rather you were told where you could pick it up and how often to take it, and sent on your way.

Since that time we have come to understand that doctors are also human beings. And while we are grateful for the specialized education and extensive training they receive, we also know that we bear a substantial responsibility for our own health via our choices in care as well as our lifestyle preferences.

Truth be told, the reality between doctor and patient is closer to that of a car mechanic and a driver. None of us think to swing by the garage when our car is running fine. It is only when we hear a knock in the engine or it is cranky turning over that we make an appointment to take it in. And while a skilled and trusted mechanic is a wonderful ally, we don't think of them the same way we do our doctors.

In some ways they are closely related. To begin with, most of us are as lost under the hood as we are when the doctor begins talking about muscle groups. We trust our mechanics to properly diagnose the reason our Chevy is sputtering the same way we want the doctor to figure out why it hurts when I do this with my arm.

My point is that while I treat my mechanic with respect, when he tells me I can't have my car back for three days when I only brought it in for tune up, I ask him what the hell happened? I don't look at his wall for his diplomas first. There is straightforward communication taking place because I hired him to fix my car, and there are some expectations that go with that process.

One of the things that sidetracks us in getting medical care is that the system can be intimidating for some people. But in the end, the doctors and the staff have jobs just like your mechanic, only they go to a clinic, or an office or a hospital and fix people and not to a garage to fix cars.

All I am suggesting is that we as a society have elevated medicine to a level of respect that can lead to patients feeling intimidated. And that is no way to gain the best treatment for you or your loved one.

Rule Number One is not to be intimidated in seeking treatment or asking questions. You and your insurance company are paying for it to be sure, so look for a level of service.

Rule Number Two is keep your ears and eyes open for how things work and who the key players are in any medical office or nurse's station. Identify people who are getting things done and are approachable.

Rule Number Three is to make friends. Forge some relationship, even in some small way. Overwhelm them with manners and kindness.

Make a positive impression on them and you may find the navigation through the maze easier.

On the other hand, sugar can sometimes come up short. Once in a blue moon, you may find that you have to push a bit to get the information you are looking for. Be respectful, be polite and be direct.

Once you know your doctor, nurses or staff a bit more, make it personal. Ask them how their day is going, not in a phony way but as somebody who cares about people. Hospitals can be difficult places to work. The hours are long, patients don't feel well and the pace and stress can often times be overwhelming. But inquiring about their health, their family or simply showing that you care can make their day and help them remember you and your loved one.

Modern medicine is full of tough days. If you can help lighten somebody's day, they are likely to remember you. And having a guide through the jungle isn't a bad thing at all.

Rule Number Four is that you can't do it alone. Bringing along a member of the family or a trusted friend to appointments can make sense. Sometimes a different pair of ears or eyes can pick up something you have missed. They don't have to wade into the conversation or advocate for a certain kind of care, they just have to pay attention.

Rule Number Five is about taking notes. Earlier I talked about notes in general. Now let me be specific. Write down questions in advance of the treatment or appointment. Organize a binder and separate it into subject areas such as medications, treatments, doctors and specialties. While the act of taking notes can distract you from catching everything said, it can also prompt important questions and the act of taking notes will cause you to be more in touch as a caregiver.

Your notes can also give you a frame of reference and a record as treatments or drug regimes change, helping you to better understand progress being made and how changes are taking place.

Chapter 5

A CAT Scan Under the Tree

In the Bay Area the seasons change in the most subtle ways. The leaves really don't turn, not like they do on the East Coast. Sure the mercury drops a little, but there is no bone chilling cold. The one thing that does take place is the days grow shorter. By the time we got back from Texas, winter was dropping hints that it was on its way.

Margaret's appointment with her doctor for her first exam was on December 9th. Nothing out of the ordinary was found, though she still had the sensation of "being full." A sonogram was set for December 12th but it too turned up nothing. One hour after we returned from the hospital we received a call at home saying they had made a mistake. They said the reason that Margaret felt full was because she had fluid collecting in her abdominal cavity.

With Christmas quickly approaching, we now knew there was a reason for the way Margaret felt. What we didn't know was why her abdomen was filling up.

Three days before Christmas, Margaret was brought into the emergency room and a CAT scan was done in the early afternoon. We waited, alternately hoping for the best and dreading the worst. The minutes stretched into hours and hours never felt so long. Margaret was terribly uncomfortable as her belly was distended. At 6 pm, the emergency room doctor came back with the test results.

The exam revealed a large tumor on Margaret's pancreas. The tumor was literally spitting out cancerous cells spreading the insidious disease and creating more tumors that affected her liver, as well as the lining of the abdominal cavity. Another tumor was found on her bladder. Additionally, her abdominal cavity had filled with two and a half quarts of fluid.

The doctor said quietly, "I don't have good news. This is not good, I'm sorry." He suggested an oncologist right away. Margaret and I both lost it, crying and holding each other. At that moment, we were both entering a world full of fear and pain. It was a world requiring knowledge that we did not have, luck we didn't seem to posses and faith in doctors and nurses whom we did not know.

I remember one nurse in particular, after we got the bad news. She was very short and she came over and gave us a hug, having to reach as high as she could to get it done. Though the hospital staff was very comforting, we needed to be alone to begin to sort out this new world. Margaret was moved to a private room and we began the heartbreaking job of calling our families.

Later, when both of us were emotionally exhausted, more wrung out than calm, Margaret looked at me and said, "Merry Christmas and I'm glad I'm the first one to go."

The words seemed to bounce around the room as I struggled to find the right way to respond. What do you say when the person who is the center of your life says those words? "Hey, one day at a time," I said.

I think in our hearts, we both knew that this was not something that we were going to get past. The reality was that this cancer was likely to end Margaret's life. Neither of us was ready to talk about that.

Margaret didn't sleep well that night. The staff set me up with a spot in her room where I could sleep, though I think I spent more time in the hall outside her room, crying. I made it a point not to cry in front of her, I felt as if she had so much to deal with she certainly didn't need to see me break down.

They didn't drain her stomach until the next day and a few visitors came by to see Margaret. We did have a strange experience with a social worker who seemed to be roaming the halls. She seemed to think that we were having a tough time understanding the gravity of our situation. I think she said something like "It's all over; you really ought to know that now."

Neither one of us knew what to make of her nor her overwhelming need to be honest with us.

We also had a visit from a clergyman affiliated with the hospital. He wanted to pray with Margaret, but I took him out into the hallway. I looked at him and said, "She believes in God, but she doesn't practice in a formal way."

He dropped his head and looked apologetic. "I'm sorry I came in," and he walked away.

We made it home in time for Christmas Eve to spend the holidays with our family. It would be a Christmas that none of us would forget.

Margaret's Diary

My wife Margaret kept a diary off and on for a number of years. Like most people who keep a diary, Margaret's entries reflected the many things that might happen on any given day.

I wanted to include some of her entries in this book so you could hear her voice as well as mine. The days I have included are from 2008, shortly after Thanksgiving, after we discovered what was wrong with Margaret and what we were facing.

Day 5 — Since the world turned upside down. Tummy is getting big again. Thoughts flying thru my mind in every direction.

Several times in last few years wondered how this whole thing was going to play out.

Day 6 — Bad day today, tummy very full — hope I can get it drained tomorrow. God, what has life become when thoughts surround the next draining? And so one fades into obscurity. Like an aspirin dropped into a glass of water.

My tummy reminds me of that old movie about aliens. When they are born—they pop out of humans bellies. I have an alien in my tummy eating me up inside.

Seems like the computer in the brain is about to crash. So much to process and try to make sense of—no wrong not make sense of—just try to figure how to go from here.

Big Xmas present this year. Cancer—not only cancer, but pancreatic cancer. The big one—the mother of all cancers.

If these are my "feel good" days and the worst is still to come (which I know is true) then I need to find Dr. Kervorkian.

Poor D—feel so sorry for him. I feel like I'm sucking him dry. Sucking out all of his strength.

So moved and surprised at the visitors and well wishers who came to the hospital on day 2 and 3, Don Curry just stood by me and held my hand. Vicki, Helen and Al from the office and John Stuber, dear friend. ER and C so sweet and supportive. Lots of tears.

So little energy. Have to really push to go out. It's so hard to dress or rather to find clothes that fit over this belly and look nice at the same time.

Beloved D. So very lucky to have him while I pass through the next several months (?). Don't know how long yet but it can't be much. He's so loving and compassionate. We cry and he holds me. Those big arms around me. Those arms are comfort personified. HA, can arms be personified? Who cares?

Day 7—So my new life begins. Completely dependent on Dr's. schedules, testing, fluid draining—waiting for a phone call! Don't feel too bad—just heavy walrus-like.

I remember seeing a belly like this on Marty, Karen, and Oma before they died.

Chapter Six

Caregiver 101

"Duty makes us do things well, but love makes us do things beautifully."
—*Zig Ziglar*

Try these numbers on for size. More than 65 million people across this country are caregivers. That's roughly 29% of the population of our country taking care of a family member struck down by a disease, a disability or a severe injury. On average, our caregivers spend 20 hours a week taking care of a love one, according to the National Family Caregivers Association.

Want more numbers? How about six in 10 caregivers work in addition to taking care of someone in their family. Two thirds of those caring for loved one have to make an adjustment in their work schedule. For some, that workload becomes so great that 20% have to take a leave of absence from work.

Being a caregiver impacts your health. About 23% of family caregivers report their health as fair or poor. And it isn't just physical health that suffers. You can notice a change between the ears as well. Someplace between 40% and 70% of family caregivers show signs of clinical depression.

Those numbers are daunting.

One of the hardest things about taking care of a loved one is that most of us aren't trained to do the job. Sure we know what it's like to be sick and take care of ourselves. Perhaps you are married and know what it is like to care for your mate, or have them treating you when you are sick.

But taking care of your child or your mate when they have the flu is only vaguely related to the trials and tribulations of taking care of a loved one facing a life threatening disease or injury.

For some, it is something as simple as going grocery shopping for someone or handling laundry chores. Others might provide transportation for someone or clean the house. These are the most common tasks caregivers do.

The number of households providing care for a loved one has tripled in the last decade. In part that number is pumped up by people living longer and the graying of America. Another factor is the emphasis placed on shorter hospital stays and controlling medical costs as more and more medical decisions are influenced powerfully by HMO's and the like. Higher levels of medical care being available in more places and improvements in the treatment of chronic conditions also contribute to the rise in caregiving. Now consider that the age group of 65+ is predicted to double to 70 million people by 2030 and you have a recipe for care giving being a reality for far more of us.

Caregivers in this country look just like you and me. Over half of all caregivers for patients age 50 and over are employed fulltime. Juggling a full time job, family responsibilities, taking care of a family member and taking care of yourself is why almost one-third of all adult children who care for family members demonstrate symptoms of clinical depression. Spouses who are caregivers and fail to deal with the inherent stress have a 63% higher chance of dying than non-care givers.

So much for the good news.

The Beginning
A good jumping off point is to fully understand what the diagnosis is, since it will dictate the kind of care that will be needed. Understand-

ing includes not only the basics of how the disease works, but what the symptoms are, possible treatments and likely outcomes. For Margaret, when the doctor told us she had pancreatic cancer, we both knew enough about that form of cancer to know it was quite serious. But neither of us knew what the treatment options were, nor did we have a firm grasp of how her treatment would turn our world upside down.

Modern medicine is a highly complicated place these days, but the simplest questions are often the most effective. Asking what you should expect from the disease is a good start. Be sure the doctor or nurse with whom you are speaking takes their time to explain it all and don't be afraid to ask them to repeat something if you don't understand. Taking notes can help as you may find that during this time you will be highly stressed and your memory may not be as complete on some things. Ask what level of care is necessary at home and how much of that you should undertake from an expertise standpoint. Be clear on the best ways to communicate with your medical care providers. Some may still favor the phone while others may be fine with email.

Once a diagnosis is on the table and a few of the basics have been explored, for many people a discussion of healthcare wishes, finances and insurance may make sense. While some of this may be awkward, it does provide for an easier time planning what comes next. Depending on the nature of the illness, talking about completing a durable power of attorney and being clear about what heroic measures or life sustaining practices the patient wants can make a great deal of difference later should the disease progress quickly. For Margaret and me, her cancer was aggressive and the time we had from diagnosis to her death was just three months.

Depending on the relationship between the patient and friends and family, at some point early on, a discussion about the medical realities and the patient's wishes can improve the level of care given and ensure that everyone involved in the process is on the same page. For the most part, Margaret's daughter Dona and I took care of Margaret and our communications were simple and straightforward. When more people are involved in the caregiving, the communication as well as the expectation level becomes critical.

After a level of care has been determined, especially if the patient is heading home, it is important that any skills or training for home care occurs with a professional prior to the day care begins in the home. For instance, I had no idea how to change a colostomy bag, but this was a critical part of caring for Margaret as well as representing a potential infection danger. I was schooled in how to clean the area, how to change the bag as well as how to dispose of the old bag. Since this procedure had the potential for allowing infection and impacting Margaret's health on a daily basis, I was more than a little nervous and concerned that I learn the necessary skills quickly. I also didn't want to show Margaret that this procedure was any cause for alarm, as she had enough to worry about. That said, my changing her bag became a source of some humor as she liked to tease me about whether I was actually doing it correctly.

The next step is to do a little detective work on a local level. Find what services beyond your level of expertise or time allotment will be needed and how you can add to the level of care you need to provide. Reach out through the local hospitals or clinics to find out what programs are available. Investigate through local social services what organizations in your community can lend a hand. Sometimes a simple Google search can bring surprisingly helpful information.

Another important step is finding somebody to talk with about the inevitable stress that will arise from providing care for a loved one. I was lucky in that Dona and I ended many evenings simply talking about the day, or maybe what we needed to take care of the next day. As often as not, however, we would also talk about subjects completely separate from Margaret and her care.

The struggle to do your best at the office, to take care of your family and home and provide the care, love and attention your loved one needs is far more than a full-time job and it is easy to become completely overwhelmed. If you don't find someone to share this with, you are likely to begin falling short of your goals in all of the above, not to mention the physical and mental toll it all can take on you.

Since your goal is to give your loved one the best care possible, it is critical to take care of yourself. You will soon learn that some of the simple things you have taken for granted now become challenges. Eating right becomes more difficult because you need to make time for grocery shopping, or find a way to have the groceries delivered. Again, according to the National Family Caregivers Association, 63% of all caregivers report having poor eating habits, and it isn't because they are slipping off to McDonald's for a Big Mac. Meal planning becomes more critical as the idea of just tossing something together relies upon having something in the pantry. Cooking is not only time consuming but can become more complicated if your loved one requires a specific diet different from yours.

The kitchen needs to be clean from a simple health standpoint and that requires more time and energy. And the kitchen is just one room of the house.

Exercise becomes more daunting. Most of us struggle to find time during the day when we are healthy or only have "normal" time constraints. Now add in the care of a loved one, and most of us will quickly come to the conclusion that exercising is on the list of things that have to be sacrificed. And while that's logical, in the medium and long term, this is exactly the wrong decision for caregivers. Your health is critical to being able to care for your loved one, and if you are too tired or out of shape to help, then you have gone from being a part of the solution to being a part of the problem. Take the time to take a walk. Ride a bike to do an errand. Set up a specific time for the gym and go.

You may feel guilty about taking a few minutes for yourself, about taking time to exercise while there are lots of things on your list at home. But you can't take care of somebody else unless you have taken care of yourself. Get used to the idea that taking care of you is part of taking care of them.

I end this chapter with a series of questions that can help guide you as a caregiver as well as a list of caregiver resources. I recommend you search out your own resources locally; you may be pleasantly surprised at how much help you may have in your hometown.

- Diet: What kind of changes or additions need to be made? Do I need specific foods and do they need to be organic or is traditional OK?
- Medications: Is there a specific order or time table in which medications must be taken? Are there specific medications to avoid (either over the counter or prescription) in terms of interaction?
- Is there a specific regime to follow in terms of pain management?
- Is there specific medical equipment that must be brought into the home? Will special instruction be required to operate it?
- Along the same lines, will you need gloves, skin care items, dressing and gauze or other items on a regular basis and where can they be found?
- Are there any special instructions required for moving someone or treating them in bed to avoid bed sores?
- Will all doctors treating my loved one have access to all records and medication levels? Will they be in communication with each other?
- Will modifications of our home be required for care?

Resources:
Family Caregiver Alliance: www.caregiver.org
National Family Caregivers Association: www.thefamilycargiver
Next Step In Care: www.nextstepincare.org

Chapter 7

A New Year, A New Doctor and New Challenges

Normally, the holidays were a time of parties, shopping and travel and family with lots to do. That Christmas we just seemed to float through them as if we were in some sort of stupor.

Before we knew how sick Margaret was, I had managed to do a lot of the Christmas shopping. I was running errands and setting things up with an eye towards getting things done at a busy time of the year, not worrying about Margaret's health. At the time, we still didn't know why her stomach was bothering her. We would go out to eat, but Margaret would hardly have a thing.

We did some of the same things we always did during the season, but it was somehow "off." It wasn't that we were constantly thinking of Margaret's cancer, but it all seemed to be a slog.

It wasn't that the holiday was unhappy, far from it. We had our laughter and there were plenty of hugs and good cheer. We played games and caught up with the family, talking about what was going on in their lives.

We opened gifts. With wrapping paper and bows spilling out around our feet, we watched the grandkids open their presents. This seemed to give Margaret a particular joy. They would each take a turn opening their present and then cross the room and give her a hug.

For Christmas dinner I went to the market and picked up a whole dinner so that no one had to cook and then we reheated everything. Margaret didn't sit at the table, but rather sat off to the side a bit. She listened to the various conversations, jumping in occasionally. She particularly liked watching the grandkids at the table; they made her beam.

I kept an eye on her. There was a distance, not necessarily borne of separation but more of thoughts. She was somewhere deep in a place of her own. Sometimes she would smile but say nothing.

I don't think anybody could quite believe what was happening. I think everybody thought I would die first. After all, Margaret was the one who took care of herself, and I was the one with the aortic heart valve that had been swapped out.

On some level, we all knew that this was going to be Margaret's last Christmas, but no one talked about it. We never brought up death, we didn't need to. I kept my feelings suppressed. All I cared about was her comfort and trying to keep her alive as long as possible.

On the last day of the year, we had our first appointment with Dr. Metzger, our oncologist. He carried a fine reputation and upon meeting him for the first time, I was struck by how young he seemed. We sat down in his office and began the unsettling business of learning just how sick Margaret was and what we could do to help.

Dr. Metzger had a calm about him that was palpable. He looked at Margaret and said, "Margaret, you have Stage Four cancer." He then went on to explain the stages of cancer in a general way.

When a doctor talks about the stage of cancer, he or she is referring to the amount of cancer present and its location. Those determinations guide the treatment options. The higher the stage of cancer, the more advanced the cancer is.

Stage One cancer means the cancer is only found in one location and has not spread. Generally this means the cancer has been caught at an early stage and the patient and doctor have more treatment options to employ.

Stage Two denotes that the cancer has spread to surrounding tissue and organs.

Stage Three cancer often indicates that the cancer has migrated to lymph nodes. This often complicates the treatment, either eliminating some options or dictating that more serious treatments be started quickly.

Stage Four point to a cancer which has spread to other parts of the body. Treatment at this stage can be complicated and depending upon many factors, may be focused not on curing the cancer but rather making the patient as comfortable as possible.

With Dr. Metzger's diagnosis that Margaret was in Stage Four, this meant the cancer had moved from her pancreas to the bile ducts, possibly the small intestine and spread to other areas of her body. He explained our treatment options including an overview about how these options applied to Margaret's condition. He suggested that chemotherapy could give us nine months to a year.

At that moment, I did not know how Margaret's prognosis stacked up against other pancreatic cancer patients, I only knew that the cancer was among the most deadly types and that Stage Four was the last stage. According to the World Health Organization, the median survival following diagnosis is three to six months. The percentage of patients living five years after diagnosis is less than 5%.

He asked Margaret how her health was in general. Was she regular? She looked at him and said no. He prescribed a heavy duty laxative. "This works great, don't worry this will be fine," he said.

Chapter 8

Friends, Family and
Other Challenges

"Love makes you do strange things." —*Charlie Brown*

One of the first reactions from friends and family when they hear someone has a serious illness is to ask if there is anything they can do. This of course is also the right thing to say and some people say it for that precise reason. Others actually mean it and some will even expect an answer.

For an even smaller percentage of people, they will ask if they can come by and visit. This generous and genuine offer also comes with some built-in challenges for both the patient and the caregiver.

Those facing a life threatening illness need contact with those they love and downtime and sleep. They need socialization and the connection to a life that is as regular as possible, balanced with the need to bank rest and energy so the body can fight the illness.

Margaret was diagnosed on December 22nd and that night we spent time on the phone talking with friends and family about what we had learned. The next day people began calling to come by and say hello. At first, the visits were welcomed and Margaret was cheered by the company as friends stopped by to visit. Inevitably, after they left,

Margaret would remark that it was certainly nice that they took the time to come by. She was behaving as she always did, she would entertain people and present her social side as soon as someone stepped into the room. There was never any hint that she felt badly or that she was tired. She felt that as long as people went to the trouble of coming over, she needed to do her best to welcome them.

Our experience might be a little different from other peoples in that Margaret's cancer was so aggressive and fast moving. On Christmas Eve, just two days after she was diagnosed, she sat next to the dinner table, but she really didn't eat. She talked and followed the conversation around the table, but already the disease was taking a toll.

In the following weeks, people would come by, in particular friends with whom she worked with at Fireman's Fund. I would greet them if I was home and I would do my best to explain to them how Margaret was feeling and what her condition was like.

The reason for filling them in was simple. If I could answer some of their questions, then Margaret wouldn't have to and she wouldn't have to spend that energy. Also, when dealing with a disease as insidious as pancreatic cancer, there is some inherent discomfort with how people ask questions, and in turn, what some of those answers are.

Generally when people stopped by, they of course wanted to catch up with Margaret, but sometimes there was an awkward quality to the conversation. They were curious about her condition and how she felt, but they didn't want to pry. They wanted to communicate that they cared about Margaret, but at the same time, they also didn't want to be rude. They knew that there was a line out there somewhere. On one side was genuine human caring and curiosity, a need to comfort a friend, a desire to help. On the other side, was a slight discomfort, a nagging feeling of being pushy or awkward.

So in some cases, people would simply come by and tell Margaret about their lives, rather than risk somehow walking across that line that they could not see or sense. I think on some levels this may have struck Margaret as odd, but she never complained about the one sided nature of the visit.

When Margaret was in the hospital, people brought flowers and she talked like a magpie, never giving her friends any sense of the pain or the troubles that she had. The simple truth was that Margaret didn't want to scare any of her friends, so she kept her complaints to herself.

Even before she got sick, she disliked talking about feeling ill or for that matter, feeling pain or nausea. And once she had cancer, she became more tolerant of the pain. This was ironic in that she had more pain to deal with and as she became more ill, more drugs to help her deal with the pain.

It wasn't until mid February that having visitors became more of a challenge. She was weaker as the cancer dug in, and her days shifted as she needed more rest. I did my best to keep her friends in the loop as they called, and there were times when I had to tell them that a visit on that particular day wasn't a good idea.

Margaret would get the biggest kick out of some of the things that people brought as her visitors carried in little "care packages." Friends continued to bring flowers as many knew that she loved her time in the garden. Others brought little things like sweet smelling soap or a book to read. One friend took to bringing little crackers or a pair of socks.

As time went by and Margaret's condition became more serious, the visitors became fewer and farther between, and everyone related differently to her as well. The visits became more centric to how she felt, more reactive to the situation and the day.

While people are often anxious to demonstrate their friendship by visiting, there is also a discomfort that some people find with seeing old friends who are no longer really themselves as a disease truly takes hold and the physical condition deteriorates. No matter what the friendship has been in the past, sometimes even the best of friends struggle with a visit or the reality that their pal is slipping away. Margaret had a couple of her very good friends visit regularly, but another close friend never came by, for whatever reason.

I found that I struggled to a small degree with her visitors as well. I wanted Margaret to stay in touch and to be as connected as she possibly could to her life as she had known it. At the same time, I was also very defensive of her condition and wanting her to feel as well as possible. It seems that I too was looking for that elusive line between what would make her happy and what might tax her body.

For my part, I tried to take my clues from her and how she felt. If she was having a good day and her energy was up, visits seemed to make sense, especially since she enjoyed her friends. When she was struggling, it was easy enough to know that having her lie in bed listening to somebody else's worries wasn't a very good prescription.

It was the days in the middle, where she seemed to be someplace else that had me guessing.

My best advice is to set up clear ground rules with friends regarding visits. Let them know that they are always welcome to call and that their company and energy are valued. Likewise be honest and tell them that some days a short phone conversation might be the best thing. Make suggestions about what they might want to bring if they ask. If your patient is uncomfortable talking about something, clue your guests in.

We have all become used to the idea of information being all around us, so sharing what you can with friends and family on behalf of your patient to make visits smoother simply makes good sense.

One way to keep in touch is to use Caringbridge.org. It is a website which allows caregivers and patients to put a plug-and-play website together that friends and family can access easily to keep up to date with the course of an illness and changes in care. It is simple to set up and allows both the patient and the caregiver to spend less time answering phone call or emails and allows people to stay in touch.

Chapter 9

A Week of Laxatives

"Optimism is the madness of maintaining that everything is right when it is wrong." —*Voltaire*

When a highly trained doctor who is expert in treating cancer says you have Stage Four cancer, you know that life has become quite serious. You begin to spend lots of time and energy learning all that you can about the disease and what might come next.

You also spend lots of time trying not to worry about what comes next. Along the way, you figure that the everyday stuff is going to need to take care of itself, the minor parts of life are somehow going to be fine because when it is Stage Four cancer, pretty much everything else falls into the minor category. You realize that you only have so much energy to begin with. You have only so many hours in the day to spend trying to make your mate feel better, to learn more about the disease, and to prepare yourself and your family for more of the same the next day.

So when your doctor turns to the woman you love and asks "how is your elimination?" it seems like one of those standard questions that they ask about a patient's general health. In light of the serious nature of the cancer she was facing, it also sounded like the old joke about John Wilkes Booth assassinating President Lincoln in the midst of a play. "So

Mrs. Lincoln, besides Abe getting shot, how did you enjoy the show?"

When Margaret told him that things in that department were not moving along so to speak, the doctor told us not to worry. He would write a prescription for a serious drug and that would take care of the problem.

This only seemed fair, if anything in this situation could be fair. With a vicious cancer attacking Margaret, the idea that an everyday thing like going to the bathroom could be a problem just seemed wrong. And of course, the doctor didn't seem concerned. He said that the laxative he was going to give her would take care of the problem very quickly.

Margaret was happy to hear that the new drug would act fast as she was fairly uncomfortable, between her abdominal cavity filling from the cancer and the constipation.

We picked up the new drug and headed home and waited. As we were both learning, so much of treating this disease and measuring Margaret's health revolved around waiting. The God Damn waiting, at times I wondered if all the waiting didn't somehow cause more problems. Did the waiting bring on the constipation? Did the waiting make it worse? Maybe that doesn't make sense but that's how it felt.

Each morning we would wake up and I would ask, "Anything happening?"

And each day, her answer was a shake of the head or a frustrated, "No, nothing."

While this was frustrating from the standpoint of the problem not being solved, there was a much larger concern. Imagine being told that you have cancer, a cancer that will likely end your life in a year, and that isn't even your main worry. Instead your chief concern is that your stomach is filling with fluids and your bowel is filled as well and you feel terrible.

This is what our life had become. I couldn't watch Margaret feeling that way anymore. I called the doctor and told him it had been a few days and nothing was happening. I asked him if there was a different drug we could try or some other treatment?

At this point, we all thought the constipation was somehow related to her cancer. Margaret and I were following orders, still basically reeling from the cancer diagnosis. We were not asking too many questions, really struggling to absorb what the illness meant and what we would do. The reality was that the deep worries about the cancer were sitting on our shoulders, especially Margaret's. I worried about her. She was so emotionally strong, a rock in the way that she seemed to handle difficulty so well. But, these were a brand new set of struggles, literally life and death, and I was concerned that dealing with it all was taking a toll.

Our doctor was surprised to hear that Margaret still wasn't going to the bathroom, "We never have a problem with that drug and it always works quickly. We use it in the hospital with great results. If it isn't working, there may be a different problem. I want to bring Margaret back in and run some tests."

On January 3, after pushing, we got the doctors to drain her belly so that Margaret could begin to feel better and we could have some of the pressure relieved. The doctors asked if the laxatives had worked and the answer was no. I remember thinking that here she was facing a most deadly cancer and the doctor had told us that at best she had a year to live. I wondered what else could go wrong, but I didn't want the answer.

Four days later, the doctors scheduled an ultrasound test of her bowel and gave her more laxatives, and still no luck. Two days later, we were in getting her belly drained again. It was becoming a regular commute and Margaret was still feeling bad.

On January 12, she ended up in the emergency room after being given an even stronger laxative. After the nursing staff checked her bowel, there was nothing there, and we were sent home.

That week, Margaret had already been to the hospital twice to have her abdominal cavity drained, so we felt like we were practically commuting to the hospital as if it was the office. To this point the only thing they had done was a CAT scan, the exam that had revealed the cancer.

This time they had her undress and lay down on a gurney to bring her in for the test. But then the inevitable happened and we had to wait. She was lying there, trying to make the best of things and she became cold, so I found her some more blankets.

They finally got her in for the exam and the tests revealed a blockage. The doctors met and decided the best way to handle it was to schedule a surgery to bypass the blockage and eliminate the problem.

Looking back, maybe I should have asked more questions. But the trouble was that we were not in some sort of clinical mode. Margaret and I had been somewhat bowled over by the diagnosis and at that time we were in a survival frame of mind, waiting for the fog to clear. Every day, it seemed like you wound up asking yourself, "What do I need to do to get us through today? How do we get from here to there?"

Although we didn't talk a lot about it, the truth is that we were both hoping for a miracle. And the notion of a miracle somehow turning around a deadly cancer like this one seemed more distant when every morning began with the simple hope that today would be the day when Margaret could go to the bathroom.

Chapter 10

When the World Shrinks
to Just One Room

"Sometimes all we need is a little pampering to help us feel better."
—Linus of "Peanuts" fame

One of the harshest realities of a life threatening illness is how drastically the world changes. And it can happen so quickly. One month you are celebrating Thanksgiving in the Lone Star State, and the next month you are sitting in a hospital room wondering what a test will reveal.

For a time while Margaret was sick, she was spending time upstairs in our master bedroom. The stairs themselves were not an insurmountable obstacle and she could still move around the house a bit. She had to sleep sitting propped up by a collection of pillows, but still, our bedroom served her needs and she was comfortable. But as the cancer took hold and her energy waned, it became clear we would need to move her downstairs into a bedroom off the den we called "Grandma's Room". Indeed, this was the room in which Margaret's mother would stay when she visited from Texas. The walls had paper that Margaret had picked out and hung herself.

"Grandma's Room" had direct access to a bathroom and was a few feet removed from the den. The den in turn had access to the backyard through a sliding glass door. Outside the doors lay the world she loved so much. A virtual forest of trees along with rolling hills, deer, a seasonal creek and of course the flowers that she loved.

At first, the move seemed elementary to me. I figured we would organize the room, put a few things in boxes and it would wind up being fine. I began to think about what we needed in the room. The first change had to be the bed, as a hospital type of bed made more sense. I simply took the bed that was in the room and stood it on its side against the wall, opening up the room for the new addition. But Dona, my step daughter, took one look at the propped up bed and told me it had to go. "This won't do," she said.

The fact that I had simply stood the bed up showed me that not enough was on my radar. This struck me as odd because in that time, to me, it felt like everything was on my radar. At the risk of maybe stating the obvious, I had the typical male response. I thought let's solve the problem and move on.

But what Dona was saying made all the sense in the world. She said that the room needed to be more than functional; it had to be where her mom would be comfortable.

She was talking about the importance of creating an environment that would not only work as a place for Margaret to rest, but as a place for her to live. This went beyond the basics of the type of bed and how the room would work. Dona was talking about how the room was going to feel to Margaret, how she would view the place.

So the old bed and frame were moved out of the room into storage. Bedside tables were set up in easy reach of the new hospital bed. Paths to the bathroom as well as to the hallway were cleared out for easier navigation. We looked at the walls as places to put things that were a part of Margaret's life, and not simply what kept the roof from caving in.

Dona made sure that we brought in fresh flowers to brighten the place, often times taking them right out of the garden that Margaret loved so much.

While I never admitted this to anyone, don't even know if I was aware of it at the time, her move from our room upstairs to the bedroom off the den was more than a simple move of convenience. When she was still in our room, life was still filled with many things that were normal. She would spend time deciding what she was going to wear, and to my way of thinking, she always looked stunning. Having Margaret in our room helped keep fear at bay; fear of the unknown, fear of how bad her sickness might be, fear about how much our life might change.

When Margaret was upstairs, there was something else in the room, hope. We still didn't know exactly what we were up against while she was spending time in our master bedroom, which meant that many things were possible. While we were frustrated that we weren't sure what we were facing, we also had the hope that whatever it was, we would have options and treatments that could work.

By the same token, moving her downstairs meant that hope meant something different. The trouble was that we knew she had pancreatic cancer and all of the horrors that went with it when we started putting the downstairs together. Hope took on a different form as we looked at that room. We hoped that we could make her comfortable, that some of the little things in life she enjoyed could work in the new room. We hoped she had more time and not less. We hoped we could manage the pain. And if hope changed when she came down those stairs, so did fear.

There was a fear that her pain might grow too great or that we couldn't learn quickly enough how to properly do her IV or the many other new tasks.

The pace of things changed when she moved downstairs as well. While life felt much more normal when Margaret was still in our room, once she was downstairs there was a sluggishness that had nothing to do with her, but rather, the pace of everything else. It almost felt like a shift had taken place and things now moved in slow motion.

Whether she was upstairs or down, our cats, Max and Amy, were always around and I think this was one of the consistent things that helped Margaret to be more comfortable. They always wanted to be close to her, sitting on the bed with her and keeping tabs on what she was doing. When we moved her downstairs, they adapted to where she was and she enjoyed their company.

We wanted to be sure the room downstairs had enough light so Margaret could read, and enough room so her water or juice was always within reach. There was a large window in the room that looked out to the creek.

We also needed to make room for a wheelchair, a new addition to our lives. The chair wasn't something we had to use all the time, but it did make life a little easier for Margaret sometimes. In setting the room up we needed to make space for the wheelchair to maneuver, which was something I had not factored in originally. Ironically we ended up with two wheelchairs, though how it happened is still a mystery.

The basics you never give any thought to day-to-day suddenly become more important when you are trying to create an environment and space that will work for somebody facing a serious illness. Is the room too cold or too warm? Is it stuffy or is there too much of a breeze? How do you keep the place clean without making a big deal of cleaning it, without making lots of noise? Is the room quiet enough so she can get rest, but is it close enough to the rest of the house so she doesn't feel isolated, so she is as connected as she can be?

We started trying to find the right combination of blankets for the bed so Margaret would be warm enough but not so heavy on her legs so she would be uncomfortable.

Since the bed was set up so Margaret couldn't look out of the room into the hallway and the den, we set up a portable intercom system so we could all communicate easier. It was the same type of system parents use with babies and it worked fine. Still, whenever she would call out or there was a noise, I found that I was bounding downstairs concerned that something was really wrong, panicking on the inside, while trying not to show any of that panic to her.

We had a TV in the room as Margaret enjoyed her movies, although we could also wheel her into the den so we could watch them together. We had a library of movies to choose from and I thought this helped make life seem more normal.

I found my thinking shifting in terms of not viewing her room as a place with four walls where she had to spend time, but rather I started considering it an environment. In a way this was the logical jump to make as we lived in Marin. As anybody who has spent some time on this side of the Golden Gate will tell you, Mother Earth very much rules the roost, and the love of nature, animals and all manner of organic pursuits makes everybody an environmentalist by default.

I also began moving from the practical aspects of how functional was the room to how did the room feel to her? Margaret was a person who appreciated beauty in both simple things and sophisticated settings. My once stilted thinking that had missed the most basic idea of moving the old bed out was actually evolving into how did the space feel to Margaret? Did it have enough of the things in it that she loved? Did the room feel cheerful?

Again, Dona was such a big help in shaping things so Margaret was comfortable and happy in her new place. This would be a reoccurring theme as I would frequently turn to Dona for advice, for her insights and sometimes just as a sounding board.

Chapter 11

A Very Unkind Cut

After the series of laxatives failed to make any progress, Margaret's doctors set up a battery of tests to determine exactly what the problem was so we could get her on the right treatment program. But the tests revealed it wasn't just a simple matter of diet or drug choices. The tests showed that Margaret had a blockage and it was decided that the most effective treatment would be a bypass surgery, an ileostomy.

This was more than just a bit disappointing. If this was to be a journey for us, it was becoming clear that the road would be more than a little bumpy and that it was full of twists and turns as well. Again, I thought to myself that it was as if the diagnosis of pancreatic cancer somehow wasn't enough, and that somehow Margaret was going to have to face other challenges as well.

It made me feel angry and frustrated. The prospect of surgery also had me fearful of what could happen. It wasn't just that Margaret had nine months or a year to live. Now she required surgery, and the surgery wasn't even for the cancer. The surgery wasn't going to help her against the cancer, although it was critical for her general health. Having the surgery and a complete recovery would allow her to begin the chemotherapy and step up the battle against the cancer.

Maybe what I was feeling was that we had done our best to prepare ourselves for Margaret's chemotherapy and treating the cancer and now the surgery felt like it had come out of nowhere.

The doctors all said the surgery was not very complicated, and wouldn't be life threatening. But having had my own surgery I was a bit wary when anybody said surgery was no big deal. I've had aortic valve replacement surgery, so the prospect of having Margaret going under the knife as well as the subsequent recovery was daunting.

The doctors described the surgery as tapping into the small intestine, making a small incision and creating an opening where a colostomy system can be set up. The procedure is known as a bypass and it would mean that Margaret would no longer use her bowels for elimination. Instead, a colostomy bag would be used.

Even as they were explaining the surgery, in the back of my mind, I couldn't help but think, "We knew Margaret was going to die, but this isn't going to be easy."

Margaret was stoic at the news. Her reaction wasn't entirely unexpected, but in all the time we had been together, she had always been fastidious about her appearance and her hygiene. Still, she managed to find a way to make light, reminding me to pay close attention when they talked about how the bag would work and how the process of preventing infection took place.

She faced the surgery down, even when there was delay. I said, "Ah come on, we have to wait for this too?" Waiting has never been my strong suit, and watching Margaret not feeling well did nothing to help me develop patience. But she was showing me something in her approach, "This is what has to happen," was her philosophy, which was interesting because she could be a tough patient. She sometimes had a difficult time with pain.

The next move was to meet with our surgeon and get some sort of feel for the expectations surrounding the actual procedure as well as gaining some insights into what was involved in the recovery.

As they described the procedure in detail and gave us an idea of what would be involved in the recovery, they said that Margaret's chemotherapy would be put off until she was fully recovered from the surgery.

With the ileostomy, I would also have to learn how to change Margaret's bag, as well as learn how to keep the area clean and free from germs. I was assured by the staff that I would receive all the training I needed so that neither Margaret nor I would have to fret about her day to day health and the bag.

The surgery itself was to take 90 minutes and all of our doctors were confident the procedure would go smoothly and Margaret would make a recovery and transition into her chemotherapy.

Our luck continued to hold as far as waiting went, and Margaret's procedure was delayed for a bit. While we waited, neither of us betrayed any concern to the other about the wait, though I may not have hidden my frustration as well as Margaret. Dona and Dona's partner Steve were there too. The room seemed to me to be enormous. The nurses were wonderful, so thoughtful; knowing that we were all filled with anxiety over what would come next.

Finally, they wanted to take Margaret into the operating room. I leaned down to kiss her and she smiled, telling me not to worry, "It's all going to be fine." God she was strong, so much stronger than me.

Then the all-too-familiar waiting ritual began. I found myself staring at my ancient Omega watch, the gold hands creeping across the face at a pace too slow to describe. The projected 90 minutes came and went and there was still no doctor emerging from the operating room. Nobody on the staff came out to give us the comforting news that Margaret had emerged in fine shape from the procedure. The two hour mark was eclipsed and all I could think of was "What the hell is going on?" There was still no sign of a familiar face to give us news until a nurse came over and said things were going slower than planned.

Finally, at the three hour mark, her surgeon came out to tell us the procedure was finished. It seemed there had been a complication in that the spot they had chosen to tie into. The small intestine on the left side near the stomach was not working for what they needed. Instead after Margaret's surgeon consulted with the head of the department, they decided to move to a spot farther into the intestine.

Margaret was wheeled into post-op and I was allowed to see her. She may have been on a gurney in a hospital recovering from surgery, but to me she looked lovely. After the staff was satisfied with her vital signs and she was stable, they moved her upstairs. I had requested a private room for her, but there were none available. She was wheeled into a room to be shared with a woman waiting to be discharged. She was on the phone all the time, apparently talking to friends or family and none too happy with the care that she had received. We were all happy to see her discharged and then Margaret had the room all to herself, for the balance of her stay, about a week.

I fully expected Margaret to complain about the pain, but she was calm, almost docile. In a way it was like she was wearing her social face, the expression where you could never tell if there was any sort of problem because she was busy engaging you, asking you about your life and what was new.

Slowly, too slowly, we transitioned into acceptance of our new reality. We now knew that besides chemotherapy to control the cancer, we had to deal with her recovery from surgery. Part of the transition too, was that nine months to a year now seemed more like a place of hope for us, and not time on a calendar. Since I have always been the proverbial optimist, I was looking at the time we had left as a chance to share some happiness and make the best of it. As often happens in relationships, mates are attracted to qualities that they may not share in the same way. Margaret had never been the same kind of optimist that I was, nevertheless, she too looked at the time she had left as being something positive, and we could still have some good times.

Chapter 12

(With Apologies to Tom Petty)
The Waiting is the Hardest Part

*"Learn how to be happy with what you have
while you pursue all what you want."* —*Zig Zigler*

There is a reason that more and more husbands are found in delivery rooms these days, and I bet there is a factor that none of them would admit is true. While the act of child birth is beautiful and can be a moment of supreme bonding for couples, it also keeps husbands out of the waiting room.

Nice name, waiting room.

Hospitals and healthcare are all about waiting. If you are a patient, you are waiting for test results, medication, a positive reaction from your insurer, a decent bowel movement or even sleep that will not come. If you are a caregiver, you are waiting for many of the same things, not to mention explanations of treatment regiments, a doctor's visit or maybe a spare moment in which you can plot what you will do the next time you are waiting.

If there is an art to waiting, I never picked it up. Part of the problem is that I'm not a person who stood in line twice when they handed out patience, couldn't take the waiting. Another thing keeping me from waxing poetically about waiting is that Margaret and I had so little time together after she was diagnosed. While we both did plenty of waiting when she was sick, I never really thought about all the time that was going into waiting with Margaret. I was caught up in much more serious contemplations, and in many ways, trying not to think about other things.

Hurry Up and Wait

If you are going to spend time in a hospital or even at home caring for a loved one, waiting will become a part of your normal routine and it can become maddening. Like lots of other people, I run a business and part of what I do each day is follow through on various details to ensure our projects meet deadlines. The pursuit of goals measured either by a timeline or a clock become second nature. Each day has a pace, sometimes dictated by projects, other times by appointments. But days or weeks spent in a hospital pulls such a workaday structure apart.

It isn't just that the hospital or clinic is simply a different place with a different set of rules, like the idea that cell phones are prohibited. No, I think the phenomenon of waiting around for everyone and everything else is closer to spending time in a casino in Las Vegas, where the architecture dictates there are no windows and reality is tweaked by excluding clocks as well. It's kind of a parallel universe where some things don't register a second thought, like bad 70's music being played endlessly or thinking of Jell-O as a treat.

While a casino is an extreme example of reality being massaged, hospitals have a similar quality in that so much of our focus is on the disease our loved ones are battling that the day-to-day tends to shrink a little bit. For instance, often times a friend or family member will say "how are you doing?" It's a simple question dealing with the overall health of the family member in the hospital. And without even being aware of it you answer that there are good and bad days.

"How Much of Human Life is Lost in Waiting?" —*Ralph Waldo Emerson*

Part of the problem with waiting and learning how to wait in a hospital is that it's different from normal life. You might wait for the mail to be delivered or wait in line at a coffee shop, but in the end you know that you will have a handful of bills, junk mail and magazines or a latte with extra foam. But waiting in a hospital has no guarantees not only about the outcome but even that something will take place. You may be waiting for the doctor to come by and explain how a new medication will interact with others. But for any of a dozen reasons, the doctor never makes it by or the instructions to change the medication are never entered into the computer.

While the waiting can be exhausting from a mental perspective, the loose ends as I indicated above can make you a little crazy as well.

And while the waiting can be frustrating for you, it can be even more difficult on the patient. Imagine that your loved one has been on a new medication for two days, but the new drug seems to have disrupted their ability to sleep, and now after two days of spotty sleep, they border on exhaustion. You have asked the doctor to come by and talk about the new drug and its side effects, but something comes up and he or she can't make it until tomorrow. In the meantime, your wife needs to sleep and you ask the nurse to give them something to make that easier. But without the doctor to sign off on the new medication, the staff is hesitant to bring a new drug into the mix. Now your wife's exhaustion gets worse and she is now more worried than ever. You are frustrated, angry and trying not to show any of that to your mate since that will only add to her level of stress.

To make matters worse, sometimes you are waiting for what may very well be bad news. Perhaps a key test has been performed that will dictate whether an experimental treatment will be OK'd and that treatment represents the only real hope you and your mate have. As you wait you want to be positive, but you also want to balance that off so if the news isn't good you can handle that reality, especially in front of your family. So you wait for news that either might turn your world around, or be a world class let down. The minutes seem to tick away like hours and the snuggly comfortable place you built for your psyche begins to fray at the edges. Now you begin looking for ways to stay positive, acknowledging that you are a little ill at ease without letting it take complete control of the process.

You want to find other ways of keeping your mind occupied, but the reality is that you can only really think of one thing, those damn test results!

Your mind strays to the collection of pills by the side of the bed and you begin picking them up, reading the label on each one as if they are the latest best seller off the *New York Times Sunday edition.*

Your wife is asleep. Thankfully, she is finally getting some rest and you begin to worry that something is going to wake her up. You begin looking around the room to prevent such an occurrence, glancing at the other patients, their visitors and the staff as they pass by the door. Should you get up and close the door? Or would that cause the noise you are so desperately hoping won't happen? Now you think that maybe it might be better if the doctor didn't come by, at least not for a while.

The above is just one of the examples from a collection of waiting stories that seem surreal, looking back at them. I'm fairly confident that the guy who said "good things come to those who wait" never spent much time at a nurse's station hanging around for the doctor to call back.

The reality is that as a caregiver you won't change this system that demands advanced waiting skills, in part because it isn't your system to change. Instead, you can only prepare yourself and your loved one for getting through the waiting with a minimum of annoyance. Here are some ideas on how to deal with the inevitable waiting.

As a Caregiver:
- Understand the scheduling being used. Are the appointments in fixed increments? Is there a time of day when service is better or worse? Try to avoid appointments that back up onto lunch.
- Be sure to bring along anything that is going to make your loved one more comfortable while waiting. This includes medication, a laptop or iPod, books or crossword puzzles. Helping them

stay informed or entertained will help them respond better to the treatment.

- Don't over-schedule, especially if your loved one is on a chemo or radiation regime. Energy will be at a premium and if they are low already, waiting may make it worse.

For You:

- Don't forget to take care of you. What will make the wait easier for you? Is there office work you can catch up on or emails you can return? While this may seem like more work, it will make the waiting go by more quickly and perhaps allow for downtime later in the day. If you have started a good book, bring it along. I tried to always have something I could do to take my mind off the waiting.

- Keep a notebook or a pad and pen handy to write down questions for the doctor as you think of them while you wait. Or use it for "to do" lists. Again, this may seem like pushing yourself, but when time is at a premium, being organized becomes critical.

Chapter 13

The Second Scariest Word: Chemo

Just the word invokes fear...chemo. Not unlike cancer. Sadly, the two seem to go together, a lesson that becomes much too clear if a loved one has cancer. In Margaret's case, they wanted to use chemo to slow down the progress of her brand of the disease. But because of the surgery for her blockage, her chemo treatments had to be delayed until the doctors deemed her healthy enough to hold up to the strain of poisoning her body with the chemo in an effort to kill some of the cancer cells.

With TV, movies, books and the media, all of us know enough about chemo to expect it to be debilitating. We know that patients who undergo chemo treatments are fatigued, lose their hair and appetites, are nauseous and sometimes report the treatment seems worse than the disease. Like so much of caring for someone or having a fatal disease yourself, you can't understand all of it until it actually happens. Chemo is different for every patient. Their reactions range from difficult to devastating and the impact it has varies as well. Margaret was anxious about the process and the truth was we didn't know what to expect. You always hear stories about how people lose their hair with chemo. Women, of course, have a sacred relationship with their hair, because so much of their femininity is connected to it. Margaret never lost her hair so she never had to go there.

We drove down Highway 101 heading to Greenbrae for her first treatment. We parked the car and headed into the hospital and the chemo treatment room. Inside were more than a few people sitting in chairs, IV's hooked up to their arms while the drug slowly dripped into their veins.

Once we were in the room, Margaret realized she knew someone else who was receiving treatment, a friend by the name of Barbara Bates. The two them were soon sitting side-by-side, both hooked up to the chemo and IV fluids. They were chattering away like a couple of school girls, lost in conversation. Neither one of them was focused on the treatment they were receiving, both enjoying a respite from the mental strain of their disease.

The sight of the two of them enjoying each other somehow made it a little bit easier for me to deal with.

Margaret's doctors had determined her program would consist of one treatment per week for a period of one month. Then they would run some tests to determine how she was reacting to the chemo and how the cancer was being affected. Then it was likely they would order another round of treatments that mirrored her first go round. The doctors felt that by taking the chemo, Margaret might add nine months to her life. When you start measuring a life in months, when the guys in the white coats talk about adding time, you pay attention.

After the first treatment we headed back to the house, unsure of what to expect, it didn't take long for us to figure out how Margaret would react. For the next five days, she was nauseated and didn't feel well. She was also being fed by IV. At the same time, we were still getting used to her bag and the routines that went with changing the bag and cleaning it properly. We were also learning how the IV worked and how changing the needle was important.

As if that wasn't enough to try to master, we were going through a bit of experimentation trying to figure out which medication worked best to treat her almost constant nausea. Nobody I know enjoys feeling sick to their stomach, but for Margaret this was maybe worse than the cancer itself. On a day to day basis, this was certainly the case. She could be a challenging patient at times, and the nausea pushed many of her buttons. When Margaret would get sick to her stomach, she would vomit and then she would pass out. This was normal for her, even when she just had the flu. In all the time we had been married, I never knew this. She had never said anything; rather it was something I was to discover. Keeping this to herself was so Margaret.

I wanted to keep her calm and help get her through this and I found the care she was receiving from hospice helped. Our hospice nurses would check the IV, make sure her dressings were fresh and well cared for and checked her belly and the bypass. Their caring and expertise did help make Margaret more comfortable and helped me worry a little less.

The next week we got back in the car for the trip down to the hospital, though Margaret still wasn't feeling very well. This time the treatment didn't go as smoothly and after it was over Margaret felt rotten.

After the first treatment there were times when Margaret wasn't at the top of her game, but she wasn't hurting every minute either. After we got home following her second chemo appointment, she wasn't really herself.

Both of us were on pins and needles, hoping that she would begin to feel a little better. I kept thinking, "This is only for a month. If we can somehow get through this, she is going to feel better. We just have to get to the end of it."

It wasn't going to be that easy. Margaret was stoic, dealing with this the best she could, but it was a struggle. There were times when she was nauseous and had to go to the bathroom at the same time. I remember thinking at the time that this was just how things were, and it really wasn't a big deal. We just needed to get through it.

Getting through seemed to be a theme I was coming to accept. Maybe it was a way of coping. It isn't easy watching the most important person in your world fight for her life, and feel so badly while doing it. It also isn't easy feeling like there is only so much you can do, and what you are doing isn't enough. So I guess I began reasoning with myself. If we can just get through the chemo this round, she will feel better and the chemo will attack the cancer, making it worth it. Basically I was bargaining.

Dona was there lending a hand. We leaned on each other, taking turns helping Margaret, learning what each of us were comfortable with and making adjustments. Dona didn't feel confident changing Margaret's bag, so that was my department. But she was great at helping Margaret feel better and dealing with the nausea.

One day I went into Margaret's room off the den to check to see how she was doing. As I turned the corner I found Margaret standing in the doorway, and something was very wrong.

Chapter 14

Coping and Other Head Games

"Of all the attitudes we can acquire, surely the attitude of gratitude is the most important and life changing." —*Zig Ziglar*

When I was caring for Margaret, I knew of course that she was very ill and that our time together was finite. I was no longer thinking in terms of our lives stretching out before us, or of the things we might do or places we might see. I was focused much more in the moment.

At the same time, I began to see that life had become a series of these moments, caring for a loved one, no matter how little time you may have, is something of a marathon and not a sprint. This being the case, you need to find ways to deal with that reality.

Just as a marathon runner trains and builds to a certain level of conditioning, a caregiver has to find ways to effectively deal with the stress and the emotional peaks and valleys. This is to say nothing of the physical exhaustion that goes with this type of care.

For me there seemed to be stages, and to a certain degree I was focusing on understanding the stages and getting through them in the best fashion we could. For instance, when Dr. Metzger talked to us about Stage Four cancer, both Margaret and I knew that she was quite sick and that the prognosis for a complete remission of the cancer and full recovery was unlikely. But someplace in my heart and in my brain, there was a hope. It wasn't a big hope, and I never gave the hope a name. In truth, I did not dwell on this hope. But it was there all the same that somehow, out of the blue with no real medical reasoning, Margaret would beat this cancer and we would once again return to a life where we traveled, argued over politics and spent Sunday morning in the hot tub.

That hope was reshaped when we had to move Margaret from our bedroom upstairs, to ""Grandma's Room"" downstairs. It isn't that I was giving up the hope, or even that I spent less time thinking about or wishing for it. It's just that when she moved downstairs, we both knew the disease was growing stronger. Inside, though I never shared it with Margaret, my hopes for us were changing. I began to hope that the disease would slow and that Margaret would have less pain. It wasn't that I was giving up in any way. I still wished for the mysterious force that would perplex the doctors, leaving them shaking their heads as the cancer somehow vanished. But my hope took on a different volume inside me. It was a bit more rooted in the reality that was unfolding.

I found I wasn't eating very well while I took care of Margaret, and it wasn't just that she had done much of the cooking. Eating changed. It was no longer about what I felt like eating or what sounded good. Food became something I needed to keep going. It was something I had to have to take care of Margaret and to get through the day at the office.

Another thing that changed was how I was sleeping. Not having Margaret in bed next to me threw me off for awhile, and that required a period of adjustment. But it was more than that. I thought between caring for Margaret and running my office and trying to keep up with life, I should have been exhausted, and I was. But I wasn't sleeping well. My sleep wasn't right and I finally went to my doctor and talked to him about it. As it turns out, changing sleep patterns is a reaction that is not uncommon in caregivers. Though the pace of life is often difficult and tiring, it is common for caregivers to have trouble getting enough sleep. My mind didn't want to quiet down as I thought about Margaret and my business, my family and everything else that seemed to require my immediate attention.

My doctor finally prescribed some sleeping pills for me to take.

Part of the problem for me was that I wanted to stay busy, in part because I didn't want to dwell on Margaret's cancer. By being as busy as I was, I was also feeding the beast. It felt as if there was nothing that was unimportant. There was a part of me that was worried that if I didn't stay busy, I would go crazy.

I threw myself into taking care of the garden, something that Margaret and I always did together. I was pruning the fruit trees, looking over thinking I only have one more to go. There were times when I felt like I was running on adrenalin, and I would get to the end of the day and collapse in bed. And still, my sleep was off.

At the time all of this was happening, I didn't realize that my physical functions were changing. My eating as well as my sleeping habits were all evolving, and not in a good way.

I had a baby monitor set up next to Margaret's bed in "Grandma's Room", so I could keep track of how she was doing through the night. The trouble was that any sound coming from Margaret's room woke me. My sleeping was fitful, even when I was actually sleeping, I was on edge.

One of the reactions some people have when they become primary caregivers is the need to unwind with alcohol. It's easy I imagine, slipping into a habit where you have a drink to settle down since the day seems endless and the stress level can be off the charts. And then you develop a need for that drink, or drinks. I like my scotch, but I was aware that a dependence on drink is one of the issues facing caregivers. It wasn't a problem for me, but I understand how for others it could become a challenge.

There are no shortages of physical, mental and emotional challenges facing caregivers, and there are also a variety of methods for coping with them.

I found that talking to somebody about what you are doing helps. I was lucky in that I spent a lot of time talking with Dona, who was going through much of this with me. In a way we became a sounding board for each other, taking turn to a degree listening and talking about how we were doing and what we were feeling. Lots of times we would talk about other things, not about Margaret or her treatments. I never thought about what we were talking about, but looking back I know it was a valve to release some of the stress. On another level, those chats were a momentary escape from a world where cancer called too many of the shots. The truth is that I am not very good at keeping things inside, so I may not have had a real choice about talking to Dona. We had long talks about history and all kinds of things.

It wasn't just talking with Dona that helped; it was really talking with anybody about almost anything. I needed to keep the family and friends informed about how Margaret was feeling. I became something of the family oracle. Every day it seemed that I was talking to her family or friends or our girls. They would ask me lots of generic questions about how Margaret felt or what the tests showed. But there were lots of funny and off-beat questions too, and a lot of the conversations took funny turns.

I found one of the things that helped me cope with the day-to-day living was to understand more about what we were facing. Fully understanding the cancer was a method that helped me cope. The more I learned about the principles of pancreatic cancer, the easier it felt to deal with. Knowing how the cancer was attacking Margaret and in turn how we were trying to treat the cancer made me feel less stressed. In some ways it was like by my understanding the enemy, the enemy was somehow less fierce.

The nursing staff helped me cope as well. At one point, the hospice staff started talking about the danger of bed sores with Margaret. At first I thought, "Holy shit, something else we need to worry about!" But when they explained what to look for and how to deal with it, it no longer seemed like another challenge. Instead, it was something that I understood. For me, understanding seemed to give me a little tiny bit of control in a situation where I had almost no control at all.

Looking back, I now understand how important it was that I cried on a regular basis. That sentence sounds funny in my ear and it may even read funny to you. But crying with some degree of regularity allowed me to release a lot of the emotions that simply became backed up. Dealing with the harsh reality that at some point in the not too distant future you are going to lose your mate, makes it easy for your emotions to get the best of you.

So I would cry, not in the hysterical way that came after Margaret was gone. My tears seemed driven by the fear of losing Margaret, the fear I wasn't doing enough. And tears came from the frustration of living a life where so much that was so important was dictated by things out of my influence.

In the course of talking about Margaret with friends and family, we would hug and sometimes just cry. As a man, you are pretty much programmed by society that there are few circumstances where crying is OK. This may seem like a stereotype for some, especially those in a younger generation. But growing up, for men of my age, this was what we understood as true. Men were emotionally strong and we very rarely cried. The sad fact is that for some men, this may still feel true. But I know that crying helped me deal with the day-to-day pressure of trying to help Margaret fight her cancer.

Connected to the need to cry is the need for the human touch. Looking back, when friends or family would hug me, it was really a good thing. Helping Margaret battle her cancer was a hard thing, and in many ways made me feel a bit isolated. But in shaking a hand or getting a hug, I found a tremendous comfort in dealing with what was going on.

In my family we have always been huggers. On Margaret's side of the family, they were not quite as comfortable with this display of affection. The interesting thing is that with Margaret's disease and her death, her family has become huggers, too.

Lastly, here is a short list of tips to help you cope as a caregiver:

- Be aware of your physical limitations and also of your general health. You won't be successful in giving care to your loved one if you are not well.

- Each day, try to carve out a little time for something you enjoy. If it is easier, write down a list of things you enjoy and try to find something on the list each day.

- Be on the lookout for signs of depression and if you find something, contact your doctor right away. Again, you can't take good care of someone unless you take care of yourself.

- Commit to understanding the disease and its treatments. Put a notebook or binder together and keep a treatment diary. This will not only make you feel less scattered, it will also help both you and your loved one keep track of what is going on and hopefully the progress that takes place.

- Look to your family, friends and community for resources and help. When someone offers their assistance, accept it. Give them something to do that makes it easier on you and something they can handle successfully. They will feel better as well.

- Familiarize yourself with your local agencies. Quite often a good place for free info and resources is the Area Agency on Aging or Eldercare (www.eldercare.gov)

- A program that I was not aware of at the time but one that can be quite helpful is "Powerful Tools for Caregivers". (caregiver@lhs.org)

- Make exercising a habit and look at how a class that will give you both exercise and social contact can fit into your schedule.

Chapter 15

The Staph Infection

It had been a little while since I had checked on Margaret so I went into "Grandma's Room" and was shocked by what I saw. There was Margaret standing in the doorway, her eyes glazed a bit and her legs unsteady. Finding her standing up was a surprise because she needed help getting to her feet. Something definitely wasn't right. As I drew closer she seemed upset or scared. I asked her, "Do you need to go potty?"

She said yes. When I got close enough to touch her I realized that she was really warm. As I moved her into the bathroom, she was panicking, definitely not acting like Margaret. Then she vomited, almost collapsing in the process.

We got her cleaned up and took her temperature. It was over 100. We got her back into bed and took her temperature again, and this time it was 103. Our hospice nurse was due any minute and when he arrived we checked her temperature one more time. He said she was getting hotter and called the cancer center, who told us to take her directly to the emergency room at Marin General in Greenbrae. Getting her into the car was not an easy thing as she was becoming delirious and refused to let Dona and me get her into the front seat. She finally relented and we pushed her into the car.

We flew south down Highway 101 with our hospice nurse following us. Once we arrived at the hospital, Margaret didn't want to leave the car. I had to run into the hospital and ask for help. A big man followed me out with a wheelchair and stopped next to the car. He then simply reached into the car and picked her up, placing her into the chair and wheeling her into the emergency room.

The staff proceeded to take all her vital signs and put a game plan together. They determined that she had a staph infection, which explained her spiking temperature.

The doctors treated the infection with high doses of antibiotic drugs. Later, after her temperature began to drop and they gained confidence in treating the infection, they told us that if we had delayed in getting her into the hospital she would have died within hours.

Staphylococcus bacteria are fairly common and are found on the skin and in the nose of many healthy people. Normally the germs do not cause problems, but if they enter the blood stream, lungs, urinary tract or heart, the resulting infection can be deadly, especially for someone like Margaret. Her immune system had already been severely compromised by the cancer and the chemo, making her much more susceptible to such an infection.

Margaret was put in a private room in the section of the hospital reserved for cancer patients, though she still was not all the way out of the woods with the infection. As the days went by, they couldn't be sure how she had gotten the infection, although the treatment of the infection did not rest on tracing the origin. Rather, the doctors were focused on stopping the infection as quickly as possible to keep Margaret from becoming any weaker, and to give her a better chance of responding to the chemo treatments.

The infection caused her to sleep a lot the week she was in the hospital. We were back to the waiting game and hoping for the best. The infection she had developed was mild as staph infections went, however with cancer, recovery from the infection was not a given.

The staff was so giving and caring. One orderly kept calling Margaret "My Beauty." There was a gentleness to how the nurses and aides cared for Margaret and it made us both smile.

While the doctors were focused on treating and stopping the infection, the fact that she was battling cancer and had already taken part in two weeks worth of chemotherapy, influenced how the doctors approached Margaret's over all treatment.

I asked our oncologist, Dr. Metzger, to speak with Margaret's other doctors and to give us a sense of where she was and when she might be able to resume her chemo treatments. He talked to his fellow doctors and they came to a consensus. After weighing Margaret's over-all health, factoring in the infection as well as the cancer's progress and her prognosis, he talked to me.

He said it was his opinion that there was not much to be gained in having Margaret continue the chemo. Her condition, thanks to the infection was weakened, and the chemo would not only be difficult on her, but it was also unlikely to have enough impact on the cancer to make it a worthwhile pursuit. He shared this with Dona, her brother David and me.

Dona and I were accepting of Dr. Metzger's news, or perhaps more comfortable with the idea that Margaret was unlikely to respond well to more chemo. Dona and I had spent lots of time with Margaret, and we were very familiar with how she had done thus far with the chemo. We had watched as the treatments made her sick and how she struggled and fought the disease.

For David, the news from the doctor was harder to hear. He hadn't had much of a chance to be with Margaret as she faced the cancer or had the initial chemo treatments. He didn't have the same frame of reference that we had, to know how hard the chemo was on her.

Instead, what he was hearing from Dr. Metzger was that chemo was no longer a good idea, and essentially the doctors didn't see the use in pushing Margaret when her condition was so fragile.

He disagreed with the idea of not using every option we had to treat his mother and I fully understood how he felt.

It wasn't that either Dona or I were willing to give up, it was more that the chemo's impact on Margaret was so pronounced, and her doctors were now saying it was their opinion that the treatments were no longer worth it. For me, when I heard Dr. Metzger, who worked with cancer patients every day, saying that he no longer felt that Margaret was going to reap much benefit from further chemo, it seemed clear.

I asked that Dr. Metzger speak with Margaret and lay out all of the information. While the staph infection had taken its toll on her in the short term, she had bounced back. I wanted her to have all the information and to tell us what road she wanted to take.

We all gathered in the room as Dr. Metzger sat down with Margaret and pragmatically explained how the infection had affected her. He talked about her cancer, the chemo she had already done and the program that would lie ahead. He talked about the pros and the cons of continuing the chemo.

In my mind, as I sat and listened to Dr. Metzger patiently explaining where things were, I couldn't help thinking Margaret sensed that we were coming towards the end. I watched her carefully, taking in the information and considering what the doctor was saying.

He finished and the room was quiet. Dona, David and I were waiting to hear what Margaret's thoughts were, how she might want to proceed. I was willing to do whatever she wanted to do. I was also hoping that she would remember how hard the chemo had been on her.

She looked at me and said, "What do you think?"

I wanted her to do whatever she needed to do, but I could tell by looking at her that she honestly wanted my thoughts. "I think we should go home," I said. In my heart, I simply wanted to take Margaret home and love and care for her for whatever time we might have left.

She nodded, "I think we should, too."

Dona and David didn't say anything as we had this moment.

And so the decision was made, one hell of a decision. As soon as the doctors gave us the green light, I was taking Margaret back to Novato. We were going home for the last time.

Chapter 16

Laughter Can Be the Best Medicine

*"Everything is funny as long as
it is happening to somebody else."* — *Will Rogers*

There isn't anything funny about cancer, or a dozen other life threatening diseases I can name off the top of my head. And while modern medicine often gives us a fighting chance with a serious illness, we need to find ways to help ourselves cope with the illness and challenges in front of us. One of the best ways to deal with the difficult times is to look for the chance to laugh.

This may run counter to everything you face as your loved one looks at a prognosis that threatens their lives, for the reality is that such a prognosis brings with it more than its share of dark days. But finding something to smile about, or even better, to laugh about, can make all the difference in the world for them and for you.

When a loved one is battling for their life, with everything on the line, it can make for an environment that is so serious and full of tension that it presents almost as many challenges as the illness itself.

There is no doubt that treating a life threatening disease requires serious intent and an energy that is equal to the task. Maintaining that focus 24 hours a day, seven days a week is not only impossible but I would venture that it's unhealthy. In order to care for someone facing a deadly disease, you have to find a way to be at your best as often as possible. And part of that maintenance for a productive state of mind is finding light moments that help to balance the difficult times when reality and pain intrude too deeply.

When the doctor first told Margaret and me that she had pancreatic cancer, we both knew the disease was serious and that her life hung in the balance. It was a deeply emotional time for both of us. In the too little time we ended up having together, there were days and nights that were filled with difficult emotions and hard realities. But there were also times when even just for a moment, cancer was not the elephant in the room. Life occasionally dealt us a funny situation or a way to forget the disease, if for only a few moments. If it wasn't for those respites, sanity would have been a difficult thing to hold onto. The first night Margaret was in the hospital, I stayed in the room with her, curled up in a chair, covered by her robe for warmth. At some point I woke up in the middle of the night and had a slight panic that the hospital staff might mistake me for her at first glance, with the robe covering me up, and wake me up for medication. Silly moments like this help get you through the difficult days.

Having cancer lay claim to a loved one is at best a tough business. Caring for them on a regular basis is a challenge, and finding a way to care for them and coping with the reality is a tall order. Until you have spent some time sitting in a room you would give your own life to not be in, waiting for news that you would give your own life not to hear, it's hard to explain just what the sound of genuine heartfelt laughter means. But when you have been inside that dark place, trying to cure something you can't even pronounce, by sheer will, good intention and promises of future good behavior, the lightest moment begins to look like shade drenched palms, restful sand dunes and cooling pools of peaceful water to somebody wandering the desert.

Don't take my word for it. The University of Maryland has

done research on the benefits of laughter. The staff has shown that laughter is good for the heart and promotes healthy blood vessel activity. Likewise, Loma Linda University in California has also demonstrated that humor and laughter can help the heart on more than just an emotional level.

Laughter releases endorphins, which make people feel better physically. Laughter also helps improve the body's ability to use oxygen. Another physical benefit of laughter is that it reduces the levels of cortisol, dopamine and adrenalin in the bloodstream. For someone who is fighting a life threatening disease, not wasting energy on fighting the effects of adrenalin release is a positive.

Across the country, formal therapy programs for cancer patients are beginning to include specific classes with the specific goal of having patients laugh. Cancer treatment centers see the benefits of laughter for patients on both physical as well as psychological levels.

The thing about it is, you don't know where the laughter will come from. Facing down cancer is a serious thing and light moments can come from the oddest places. One day as I was in the bathroom assisting Margaret, I turned and looked at her. "Did you ever think this is how we would end up?" Without missing a beat, she came back at me and said, "I don't even think you know what you are doing."

Years ago, Robin Williams starred in a film called Patch Adams. The movie told the story of a young doctor interning at a teaching hospital who felt the traditional interaction between doctors and their patients did both parties a disservice. Instead, he desired a relationship where the professional distance sought by doctors would be eliminated and patients would be treated on a more personal level. He also believed in the power of laughter and humor to not only make patients feel better, but to help them heal. In real life, Adams founded a hospital and foundation that made his vision a reality.

Laughter reduces the level of stress for both patients and caregivers. And as anyone familiar with how stressful hospitals, doctor's offices and clinics can be, anything that can lessen that stress is worth investigating.

One of the new realities of Margaret's condition was that after the surgery, she had a colostomy bag. The doctors and staff were very good about giving me instructions as to how to care for her and take care of the bag to avoid more problems and infections. I was quite clear on the procedure, but this didn't stop Margaret from having some fun with me about it. "Do you know what you are doing? Don't screw it up," she warned, as I tended to the bag, her voice full of mock doubt. Joining in, I asked her if she wanted to give it a try.

One of the challenges facing caregivers is that for the most part, we are not experts in medicine or treatments, so there is a degree of guilt around the idea of not being able to do enough. But one easy way to help contribute to the treatment of a loved one is by raising their spirits because laughter is contagious.

Patients facing life threatening diseases often feel isolated from society at large and sometimes even from friends and family. There is a reality that no one wants to talk about. Too often patients are made to feel as if they are alone in their fight because we, as a society, are less welcoming to those who are sick. Even friends and family can feel ill at ease, unsure how to treat a loved one who is very ill or dying. We feel a pressure to not only say and do the right thing, but also to not do or say the wrong thing. Death is a very serious matter and to somehow bring levity to a situation that is grim can make most people nervous and ill at ease. But laughter and humor can help bridge that social gap and help patients feel more in touch with the world. And for those able to get past the initial discomfort of adding humor to a serious situation, the friend or family can feel better as well.

One danger facing both patients and caregivers is that the treatment of a life threatening condition or disease can literally take up all of the energy and time of everyone involved. While any doctor, patient or caregiver will agree that when facing down a deadly disease, any and all efforts must be in play, there must also be a balance that helps everyone in the process maintain the human element. For many people, laughter and a sense of humor can be that balance. Even the most mundane tasks can provide the smile or laugh that helps get you through the tough moments.

As Margaret's condition became more of a challenge and stairs proved too hard to climb, we transformed "Grandma's Room" off the den into her room. We also picked up a wheelchair to make it easier for Margaret to move around. Her new room had a small step leading into it, and no matter how many times I moved Margaret from the room in her wheelchair, she continually asked me if I was going to drop her. She had no real fear that suddenly my strength would give way, but her teasing was a way for her to lighten the moment and give me a hard time. Sometimes when I would wheel her into the garden so she could spend time in the sun or look at the flowers she loved so much, she would warn me to be careful navigating the chair. "Don't let go of me, I could wind up in the creek," she said.

I answered back in kind, "Maybe you need to be in the creek." In some ways, I think we both came to expect that kind of back and forth and it did make things more fun at a time in life when fun was harder to find.

From a psychological perspective, laughter can also keep depression in check. Any long-term or life threatening disease can bring with it a depression as both patients and caregivers consider a reality that life as they know it has been altered, perhaps on a permanent basis. Prolonged physical pain can also create depression in patients. And while laughter can't decrease the amount of pain, it can help keep debilitating depression from dominating the days of patients.

Laughter is also an emotional release and can aid both patients and caregivers in dealing with the very real emotional ups and downs that are part of a life threatening diagnosis. Bottling up emotions can lead to elevated levels of stress that impact the patient's immune system and can be detrimental to their general health. People facing a life threatening disease or those taking care of them seldom think about stress in the classic sense, when there is so much to do and not enough time in the day. Nonetheless, stress is all around us and the littlest thing can either set it off or ease the load. Shortly before Margaret passed away, when she teased me about being a dirty old man because I came into her room as she was being sponge bathed, I laughed because I had, in fact, been enjoying not only the sight of my wife, but the look on her face as she caught me looking. "What are you looking at you dirty old man?" she asked in mock horror.

And it's an established fact that a positive outlook and attitude can impact a patient's ability to make adjustments to new treatments as well as directly affect their overall health. Laughter and maintaining a sense of humor, even in the face of cancer and other life threatening diseases, gives patients a better chance of dealing with their illness effectively.

What You Can Do

Some of my suggestions can also fall under a more general umbrella of making your loved one more comfortable and improving on the overall quality of life. Oftentimes a patient's world may shrink down to a hospital room, a single bedroom or the ground floor of their home. With that in mind, creating an environment that makes laughter a viable option is a positive thing.

Create a DVD library of their favorite movie comedies. Be sure to include films that feature their favorite stars. If they are healthy enough to go on outings, consider a trip to the store to have them pick out new films, or a trip to the library to borrow something they haven't seen. If their diet and treatment allow for them to enjoy popcorn or candy, put a basket together of treats that go with the films. Simplify the operation of the DVD player and TV as much as possible and be sure to have remotes available within reach of your loved one. It's hard to laugh if you can't get the DVD to operate and the last thing that you want is for your effort at bringing laughter to the room to morph into frustration. Watch the movie with them and share the experience, especially if their illness makes operating the TV too difficult.

If they have a favorite author that makes them laugh, go to the bookstore or the library and surprise them with a few choices.

Encourage visitors to stop by who are humorous and let them know before the visit that you are hoping they come armed with a funny story or a few jokes. Talking about a shared memory that was a good time or telling a funny tale can lighten the load.

Suggest friends and family write emails or letters that are humorous. Letters can be especially meaningful since they are more unusual these days.

Find out when your loved one's favorite TV shows are scheduled and, if possible, watch with them. If they are in care at home, TIVO the shows or use On Demand features so that they can enjoy the shows when they have the energy to watch.

While laughter is not a substitute for medication or treatment, it is an important part of everyday life and can make an honest difference in how we feel and see our world.

Chapter 17

Hospice Care: How it Works and What to Expect

Almost one million patients a year elect to receive treatment through a hospice facility or service. Across the country, there are more than 5,200 active hospice programs. Yet hospice care continues to be misunderstood by many people who think of hospice as a place patients go to die.

Hospice care differs from treatment offered in hospitals or clinics in that patient care centers on palliative as opposed to curative; that is doctors, nurses and staff are focused on the quality of the patient's life and the comfort level that can be attained. While traditional medicine assumes a pyramid with doctors and nurses at the top of the structure and patient and family below, hospice care tends to be more personal and related more closely to the needs of the patient and family.

For us, hospice care was not a substantial change at home because for the most part, either Dona or I was around and we didn't require that much help. However, once we made the decision to take Margaret home, the hospital staff suggested we meet with someone from hospice.

A counselor came to the hospital and met with us to introduce us to how hospice worked and how it could help Margaret. The representative described how the caregivers worked with patients and their families. They explained about counseling options that were available to all of us, including therapy and spiritual counseling. They went into detail about how nursing would work. They gave us contacts and after we came home, we began our hospice program.

Hospice nurses and caregivers would come by on a regular schedule to not only check on Margaret and how she felt, but also to look at the care we were giving and to help us do a better job. When Margaret first came home, she was being fed a special liquid diet intravenously through a tube connected to a permanent port in her shoulder. The changing of the food supplies was a tricky situation that required sterilizing all surfaces.

Dona became very good at the procedure, but we were always worried about the chance of infection. We were constantly checking to make sure that Margaret's temperature was on the cool side, as she could not tolerate a high body temperature.

While hospice care is a noble idea and you will likely find your staff is empathetic and hard working, you may encounter some hospice nurses can be aloof. While this kind of work can be rewarding, it can also get to people. The majority of the hospice nurses we encountered were helpful and instructive. They often pitched in lending a hand with changing sheets or bathing Margaret. They kept in regular contact with us via the phone.

On the day that Margaret passed away, we called hospice to have a nurse verify the death. The nurse who arrived at our house was new to us, which could have been awkward. Instead, she was professional and comforting, helping us through a difficult time.

The concept of hospice has evolved since the 11th century. The idea of hospice grew in popularity in Europe, with it gaining a higher profile with the work of Cicely Saunders in the United Kingdom during the 1970's. From there, hospice hopped the Atlantic in terms of gaining a degree of acceptability in the United States. Today, a third of patients who are diagnosed as having a terminal condition receive some form of hospice care.

When putting a care plan together, hospice staff typically meets with the patient and their family and talk about care options, as well as goals. Rather than focusing on the improvement of health or the curing of a disease, care revolves around the concept of improving the quality of life the patient has left.

This can take a little getting used to as some members of the family and friends may have a difficult time making the transition from trying to cure a disease or condition to simply making the patient as comfortable and as pain free as possible.

Hospice staffs are healthcare professionals, well versed in the treatment of patients in a terminal condition. The areas they can assist with include sophisticated pain management, emotional and spiritual counseling for both the patient and family as well helping to provide a sense of community. One of the hardest things about taking care of a loved one who is facing their final days is the feeling of isolation that can become your constant companion. Hospice is one way to become a part of a larger community and lessen those feelings.

Perhaps the most unique feature of hospice care is how the negative image of death is replaced by the idea of preparing the patient and their family for death in a way that comforts them and fits into their particular situation. One of the basics of hospice care is that the entire family can participate and help to demystify death. Hospice looks at death as a natural part of the life cycle and attempts to take the fear out of patients and families facing death.

Hospice is covered by Medicare on a nationwide basis, and by Medicaid in 47 states. Additionally, most private insurers cover hospice services, so for the most part, as long as hospice is available locally, care can be a viable option if a patient or family desires it.

Even after a patient's death, many hospice programs offer a continuum of care for family members via therapy or bereavement groups.

Chapter 18

Knowing When to Say When

*"Nothing is impossible for the person
who doesn't have to do it."* —*Bumper Sticker*

When you get to the end of a book, you simply run out of pages. Hopefully the author supplies you with a finale that is true to the story and its characters and satisfies you. The same can not be said for the conclusion of a life. Fate or circumstances too often step-up to provide a twist we neither choose nor enjoy.

But modern medicine with its advancements in technology and pharmaceuticals is presenting us with opportunities to live longer lives, keeping life threatening diseases at a chronic stage for longer periods of time. This is different than eating a macrobiotic diet, exercising four hours a day and abstaining from alcoholic beverages and adventuresome behavior. That is the phenomenon of living a life that only seems longer.

At any rate, when we or a loved one end up with a life threatening diagnosis, at some point a decision needs to be made about just how far we want to go to prolong our lives. Many hospitals now have this as a standard piece of the admission packet, either in a "DNR"–Do Not Resuscitate order or in a form that allows patients or in some cases their loved ones to say which measures may be used in the event of an emergency. For some of us, the paperwork takes us by surprise, forcing us to consider things we thought might be better left for another day. For others, it simply codifies thoughts and feelings that were long ago decided.

There are a variety of factors that go into such an important decision, along with the notion of when to make such a critical determination and whether other people's wisdom and feelings should be included. For the most part, it seems to come down to quality of life vs. quantity, timing and how many people to include in the process. In this chapter we will try to take this complex question apart a bit, look at the impacts on both ourselves and those around us and give you a few ideas on how to approach this assessment.

For the record, I don't have an opinion as to what the right answers are or how to make your decisions. All I want to do is tell you what to expect so that you are better equipped to make decisions that are right for you and for your family.

Quantity vs. Quality

I'm reminded of a story a friend of mine told me about him and his sister. It seems that their father was growing older and the siblings had a difference of opinion about just how dear old dad should be living the remainder of his life. The sister felt that her father should go easy on the red meat, mix in more veggies and limit his intake of libations. The son felt that his father had worked hard, saw his share of challenges and deserved to live as he chose. He argued with his sister that if dad wanted a rib eye for dinner, he would be happy to grill it for him. And if his father were thirsty, he would shake him a martini. "I want Dad to live a long life, I can't imagine what life will be like without him, but he has earned the right to live as he wants. My sister is interested in his living longer, but what about what he wants?"

It may not have been that simple, but it does illustrate both sides of the classic philosophical question of which is better, quantity of life or quality of life? This debate has raged in one form or another for generations, but it is the larger question that is more interesting. It seems to me it isn't about which is better. Each person must answer that for themselves and whatever answer we arrive at is the right one for us. But the matter of how to make such a determination and what ingredients go into such a decision is something that is easier for us to get our arms around.

Our preferences are at least influenced by society. In America, we are raised to believe that for the most part, more is better. The Fortune 500 are celebrated for their ability to put vast personal wealth together, while a list for those of us who struggle to find our ways financially has yet to be placed in a national magazine. The Playboy Empire was built on the simple notion of displaying pretty women who are well endowed. And at every turn we are bombarded with opportunities to Super Size that for just another $1. After all, more cheap food must be better.

These societal examples may seem a bit simplistic when we are considering a decision involving just how far you want to go to keep on living, or helping a loved one do that. But maybe understanding the world we live in helps us understand how we view it, and how we see ourselves in it. For example, there may be small things we do in life that give us indicators where we come down on the larger issues.

One of the reasons for collecting wine is to cellar it so that we can open and enjoy when it is at its best. Yet how many of us know people who save that bottle for the perfect occasion but never seem to find the moment worthy of uncorking that wine? If you find yourself in the school of thought that the bottled masterpiece can only find its way into glasses if the night is perfect, then maybe the idea of living as long as possible is a bedrock value you have and the debate of quantity and quality isn't such a question.

On the other hand, if you look at that same bottle of wine and see it simply as something for you to enjoy with friends or family, maybe you come down on the other side of the issue.

A scene from the film Sideways illustrates this particular example. Miles, a paranoid uptight writer collects wine and lets an acquaintance know he has a particularly wonderful vintage being saved for the perfect moment. She opines that the wine is simply wonderful and enjoying it anytime would be worthy of the grape inside. What, she asks him, are you waiting for?

The next scene shows him sitting alone in a fast food joint slugging down the wine out of a plastic cup alongside his burger and fries, satisfied with both the wine and with himself for stepping outside his comfort zone.

Of course there are so many factors that go into the debate when you begin thinking in terms of the end of a life. For example, a parent facing a decision about what kind of measures to take to keep living might look at the wedding of their youngest child as a reason to pull out all the stops. A fear of death would certainly make the debate easier in choosing the quantity side. A professional or personal goal left to achieve might help tip the scales in favor of taking measures to stay alive. Whether it is a simple "bucket list" or a lifelong wish, that thing left undone could be more than enough for somebody to draw up papers saying that all measures would be taken to preserve life. Perhaps the least emotional and most pragmatic reason one might decide to leave no stone unturned, would be the concept of a cure becoming available. While we have found many ways to treat diseases or even cure them over the past 20 years, there are still diseases that when the diagnosis is made, we are told there are treatments but no cure. It is truly a human reaction to hope that research leads to a cure and that the timing will be such that you or your loved one will benefit.

More practical medical reasons may sometimes rule the day. If the administration of a treatment or drug would present a whole different set of challenges, doctors or hospital staff may not consider their use. Or if a treatment would put you or a loved one in the position of having a side effect so daunting that the original disease or condition almost seems like a blessing, it may be easier to say let's not go down that path. If the fight for life has already been so difficult, perhaps one feels the quality of life has reached a level where there really isn't much of an argument.

Another reason one might take refuge in the idea of quality over quantity is how fighting a disease to the bitter end will affect the rest of the family from a financial standpoint. Although the world of healthcare is in the midst of shifts, it is still a world that is quite expensive, even with high quality coverage. Paying a fortune to keep yourself in a condition where every day is a new experience in pain may not be what you want and it may make life more difficult for your family.

Quality or quantity may come into play for some when they consider how hard it can be for a family to watch a loved one suffer without much chance for recovery. It may sound cold, but a long illness absent of honest hope takes a toll on everyone in a family.

So determining where you or a loved one wants to draw the line in terms of heroic measures is a key decision to make, and finding out how one answers the quantity vs. quality question can bring the issue into sharper focus.

A Few Words about Fear

When it comes to battling deadly diseases, there are plenty of things to fear. To begin with there is the simplest fear that we have, the fear of dying. We make decisions every day on a variety of things based on the idea we would like to be safe and alive. When we are faced with the reality that dying is no longer about driving too fast or getting on the wrong airplane, the fear of dying can drive our decisions about what measures to take to stay alive. Along those same lines, we can also feel a fear of losing someone and that fear can influence how we look at measures to battle an illness. These fears are very human and very common, and admitting they are there can help us deal with them as we look at the larger issue.

Timing

Making a decision before anybody's health reaches a critical juncture is far better than trying to make a decision in the midst of an emergency. Having the ability to weigh options, speak with people you trust, or even simply weigh options in your own mind at a relaxed pace can remove some of the stress and angst such a decision can bring.

It isn't just the timing of when you consider the decision that can be difficult for a family; it is also when you or a loved one decides to share that information. Many people fret over how or even if they let people in on what many people consider a profoundly personal decision. The trouble is that should you or your loved one keep it to yourself, other family members may be caught off guard by what you have decided. And, since they have not been informed of the decision, it may come at a highly tense time and cause difficult feelings in moments when emotional support can be crucial.

Explaining your decision or that of a loved one at a time when people can hear what you're saying, can make receiving the news much easier.

Another aspect to bear in mind is that while you or a loved one may have struggled with this decision, you may be surprised at the relief that some family members experience knowing you are at home with that decision.

This is by no means a guarantee that everyone in the family will embrace the decision. But the fact that it is out there and has been discussed can transition it from something people have quietly thought about and possibly dreaded, to a subject that is no longer closed off or taboo.

Who to Talk to?

Like everything that we have already talked about, there is no easy answer here. As many good arguments can be mounted regarding keeping your own counsel as opening the process up to a variety of people. Rather than try to convince you that one approach makes more sense than another, let me again simply give you an idea of different reactions you can expect from people.

If you are of the school of thought that this is the most profoundly personal decision that one makes, and as such you wish to keep your cards close to your vest or only share your thoughts with a very small group of people, so be it.

On the other hand, if you are close to your family and you make this decision on your own; don't be surprised if there is some discomfort when you make your wishes known.

If you want to seek out different opinions, be specific about what the question is and present a timeframe for the discussion. Pick a quiet private environment for the discussion and choose one person to lead it. This is a sensitive enough topic without turning it into a debate.

Take all the feedback in and thank people for their thoughts. Bear in mind that at some point, if you ask people for their thoughts, they will expect you not only to share your decision with them, but also how you reached your conclusion.

Whatever decision you reach, it will do no good unless you inform your doctor, the hospital and possibly, your lawyer. All the well meaning research, soul searching and outreach won't mean much unless you follow through.

Chapter 19

Going All the Way Home

"Take the time to be quiet." — Zig Zigler

When Margaret came home from the hospital, there was no mystery left about what was happening. The hope against hope for more time was gone, replaced by the reality of making her as comfortable as we could, for as long as we had.

Without the illusion of more time or perhaps, of better time, life settled into a routine. We were getting Margaret up and going through the usual morning rituals. We checked her bypass bag, insured her medications were in order and gave them to her. After that, we would do what we could to entice Margaret to eat something.

At this time, Margaret was taking various anti-nausea drugs and pain medications that included methadone and morphine for when the pain was bad.

Dona worked hard to get Margaret to eat as she didn't have much appetite. Breakfast might be some sliced oranges or strawberries, perhaps some juice or even chocolate ice cream. We wanted her to eat, so anything that appealed to her was great.

By this time she was too weak to stand and take showers, so we moved a plastic chair into the stall to make her more comfortable. Since she was always happier wearing clean clothes we were careful to always have her favorite nightgowns ready for her, as well as sweats if she was cold. Her routine always included taking care of her hair as well as brushing her teeth. Even as she was dying, she would not let go of her meticulous approach to her appearance. There were so many things that I loved about her, and this was one of the traits that really endeared her to me.

Her interaction with us really depended on the drugs and how she was feeling. If she was having a good day I might wheel her into the backyard so that she could sit in the sun and soak in some rays while enjoying her flowers, the fresh air and the sounds, as the creek was still running. The daffodils, camellias and the rhododendrons were all in bloom.

When she was not feeling as well she would nap, saving her energy up for other days.

There were still days when people would come by to visit, and Margaret would do her best to rally, putting on her social face and sitting with her friends. Sometimes talking and following the conversation was no problem and she would interact. Other times she would nod her understanding and allow her visitors to carry the weight. Even with Dona and me, there were times when she would sit quietly and just listen to the two of us talking, participating with just an occasional nod of the head or with eye contact.

Since we were big movie fans, we had a library of movies and there were times when she would pick one out and we would all sit and watch together. As bad as daytime TV is, we would sometimes end up watching that as well.

At night, the routine would kind of reverse, taking her through the early evening ritual of brushing her hair and preparing her for bed.

It was a hard time for all of us, especially for Margaret. Though we never talked about her dying, she knew what was before her. The drugs made it easier for her to endure the pain, but they also made it harder for her to participate fully in her life. It was a tradeoff but not an easy one.

I struggled with how she seemed to shrink right before my eyes. She was slowly but unequivocally deteriorating a little bit at a time. She was losing weight, getting down to skin and bones. It was a hard daily reminder that I was losing the most important person in my life. I took special care not to show Margaret my internal emotional struggle. I was silently watching her just wither away, and part of me was fading away, too.

We tried to not only make her comfortable but also find treats to make her day more special. A week after she got home I had her hairdresser come in, as well as a lady to do her nails. This was a real hit with Margaret and it seemed to rev up her energy a little. "Look at my nails, Diet, look how pretty they are," she said at the end of the session.

We tried the hair and nail routine again, but this time Margaret became nauseous and we had to cut it short. After Margaret came home, the nausea was really the worst of it. This is not to say the cancer and the pain were not impacting her on a minute to minute basis, but the nausea dominated how we operated. Moreover, for Margaret, there was nothing she found more objectionable than vomiting. While she certainly struggled with the physical side of the nausea, there were times when I thought the emotional and mental toll was even greater. She sometimes felt a bout coming on and she would say very urgently, "Quick give me the medicine," hoping to cut off the attack.

While I wanted to do everything that I could to help her feel better, there were times when I simply had to go to the office. Not only did I need to get things done, but I also needed to ground myself in a reality away from the house. And the reality was that my being at home wasn't helping Margaret in the way I wanted.

She was getting weaker, her energy seeming to evaporate. Even the simplest tasks were becoming a challenge. And though I know she felt it, she never talked about death or what was to come next. It was the way she was and so it was not a conversation we were going to have.

For example, on the last Monday of her life when I entered "Grandma's Room" while Margaret was receiving a sponge bath, she joked with me about staring at her body. Though her body was failing her in a terrible way, her mind was still sharp and her heart was still full of love and humor.

The night before she died, I was helping her in the bathroom, and she kind of let go, giving out. We put her to bed wondering what it meant.

The next day I was at a business lunch when Steve, Dona's partner, called me and told me that Margaret was gone. I found myself asking him if he was sure, and he said, "Yes!"

I got home and went right to Margaret. She was lying stock-still, strangely peaceful, with her head to one side. Dona said that she had given her the pain medication and that it had been a quiet morning. She said that Margaret had taken some deep breaths and then.... nothing. She couldn't wake her up and that is when they had called me.

I kissed her forehead and stood at her side for a bit and then I covered her up.

We called the mortuary and they came out and placed Margaret in a green bag, her favorite color, to take her away since her journey was now over.

I got on the phone, calling everybody in the family, beginning with my kids. I called my office and my partners, Al and John, came over to say goodbye. Steve, Dona and I talked for hours it seemed, though I don't have any idea what we said. I was dazed and bewildered and lost. The doctor had told us at the outset that it might be nine months; maybe a year, but it had only been three months. Still, it wasn't like I didn't know that she was dying and that she was getting weaker each day. And yet, I was shocked when it happened. I was numb and it seemed there was no limit to the amount of tears I could shed. All I kept thinking is "what do I do now?"

John and Al were there and we talked about life I think. There was a lot of hugging, and at some point we walked outside. I looked around the garden that Margaret loved so much and I realized all the Daffodils were dead. I said something about their death and John offered, "That is what flowers do, Diet."

All I could do was shake my head, "Not all at once," I said.

They had been blooming on Monday and on Thursday they were gone. I didn't know what to make of that then, and I'm not sure that I know now. But there is a part of me that can't help but feel the flowers died of a broken heart.

I certainly knew how they felt.

Chapter 20

Saying Goodbye

A light rain was falling early that Saturday morning and the sky was overcast despite it being May. It would prove to be the last rain of the season and that was poetic in that Margaret loved the rain. All week it had been windy but today the air was still and heavy, pungent with bay leaves as if Margaret herself had ordered the weather. The creek was running below the house and I stood for a bit and listened.

I couldn't sleep. I was nervous about the weather, I was nervous about the preparations and whether people would be there. Though Margaret had been sick for three months, I still wasn't ready to say goodbye. She was the love of my life and a life without her was something that I wasn't ready to think about. I had no idea how I would face a church full of friends and family.

I walked through our house, the house we built together. Despite some of my family being inside these walls waiting for Margaret's service, the house still felt a little bare as I went around and woke people up, getting my stepson David and his wife Jana out of bed as well as their daughter Megan. Burning nervous energy, I checked outside on the tent that ran the length of the driveway, and the tents on the back deck. The chairs and tables and even the sound system had been set up the night before. We had heaters in case the weather turned cold. Down the driveway I looked to see if running water was coming across, afraid the weather might make it hard for guests to move around.

It's funny what you remember. Jana couldn't find her belt and I offered her one of mine, as if it would work for her. She found her own and I went back to worrying about things I couldn't control like the weather and my emotions.

Margaret's favorite flower was the Texas Bluebonnet and I had taken time that morning to go over to South Novato Boulevard and pick some that were growing wild, giving them to Margaret's son David. We had a private internment at Valley Memorial Park before the service at church.

At the cemetery, we gathered around the grave. I was holding Margaret's remains along with a yellow rose. The Pastor talked for awhile, but I have no idea what he said. I can remember thinking "Why is this happening?" unable to focus on what he was saying and unable to answer my own question. Finally, it was time to put Margaret in the grave and I hesitated, seemingly unable to bring myself to let go. After a moment, I handed the box to George from the cemetery staff who placed it in the grave. I got down on a knee and placed the rose on top of the box.

At that point it all came tumbling out. All of the confusion, my grief, uncertainty and worry gave way. The tears overwhelmed me and I began to shake uncontrollably. My daughter Erica, held me and helped me to my feet. David put Margaret's bluebonnets in the grave. Suddenly it seemed as if the whole family was hugging and crying, holding each other as if we let go, things would fall apart. For me things had already fallen apart and I wasn't sure how, or if, I could put them back together again.

Reaching the church not far from home, my worries about the weather keeping people away were relieved. Though the old line says that the turnout for a funeral pretty much depends on the weather, more than 200 people turned out to say goodbye to Margaret. Many came from a good distance and one of my good friends arrived despite the fact that he had lost his wife the day before.

Because the church holds just 150 people, we set up a video system in an adjoining room so that everyone could be a part of the service. I was the last person to be seated, taking a spot next to my youngest daughter.

While my emotions had overwhelmed me at the cemetery, now I was numb. The service began with the Pastor greeting everyone and launching into the ceremony. Judy Arnold, an old friend of ours and a county supervisor, spoke at my request, talking about Margaret's Texas roots. She knew as well as anyone how independent Margaret was. Judy touched on Margaret's accomplishments, including her obtaining a college degree while raising three children. My wife was quite educated having earned master's degrees in both English and German Literature from UCLA before we met. She spoke of Margaret's work educating low income kids in Southern California, something she was quite proud of. She spoke of Margaret's smile, a smile I fell in love with when we both worked at the Marin Municipal Water District. Judy pointed out that Margaret always had a wonderful sense of style, and gave me credit for buying all of her clothes.

As Judy spoke, I kept thinking of Margaret and was still not sure that I could bring myself to speak. Other people talked, one of Margaret's childhood friends gave a moving speech.

Judy's speech had given me enough openings to say a few things so I took a chance with my emotions. I stood in front of all of those people, our friends and family, and started by noting the weather and the fact that Miss Margaret would have loved the rain. I thanked everyone for coming and noted that Judy had certainly gotten it right when she said Margaret was independent, to which I added, "Very."

I always felt as if both Margaret and I had our own worlds, but also our own world together. I lifted a line from Bill Cosby, "For two people to live together day after day is unquestionably the one miracle the Vatican has overlooked." People laughed and I added, "We had our own miracle together."

Judy had pointed out that in some ways Margaret and I were the odd couple. She was a lifelong Democrat, given to supporting social causes and rooting for the underdog, while I was a dyed in the wool Republican. "But I learned long ago not to fool with the Democratic Party," I told the audience, still, sometimes I needed to be reminded. One Sunday morning prior to the 2008 election, I suggested to Margaret that it was too bad we didn't have a candidate to vote for that had John McCain's experience and Obama's charisma. I recounted to the church full of people, "But I crossed the line. She didn't talk to me all day. It wasn't until 5 o'clock, when I poked my head into the den and asked if she wanted a glass of wine, that she uttered a word. All she said then was, "YES!"

I talked about Margaret's strength. I'm sure people expected me to talk about how she faced down the cancer and refused to give into the disease that ravaged her. She was courageous in how she handled her illness, but to me, her courage was defined by how she pursued an education in Texas, where the traditional thought was for women to have a family and stay home. She went to school, despite being told by her grandfather that "women don't go to college."

Judy talked about Margaret's wonderful sense of style, giving me a chance to lighten the somber mood. I said, "I did buy her clothes. And it was fun to shop for her because whatever outfit I picked out for her, she always looked good and classy. The problem was she wouldn't let me wear them!"

The joke lightened things up a bit. I talked about her love of plants and how her green thumb was a real gift that made our yards beautiful with the camellias and daffodils near the driveway.

Margaret loved music, everything from classical to country, having played drums and piano in her high school band. For the service, Christina, my daughter, played the piano while my granddaughter sang *Time to Say Goodbye*, a beautiful song by Andrea Bocelli and Sarah Brightman. She also sang *Amazing Grace* at the end of the service. It was uplifting and beautiful and sad all at once.

As the final notes disappeared into the crowd, the tears returned to my eyes and Erica comforted me. The family headed for the chapel entrance where we thanked everyone for joining us. People were so thoughtful, stopping to say hello and sharing memories of Margaret. One woman remarked that she wanted a program of the service to give her husband, "This is the service I want," she said.

Afterwards, we had people to the house for something to eat and drink. When I got there, I walked around to the back where the deck is and was greeted by my business partner, Al, holding a tumbler of scotch. He handed the drink to me, saying "I thought maybe you could use one of these." It was a comforting moment on a difficult day. We hugged and I took a pull on the scotch, which tasted fine.

The gathering went on until 5 o'clock, with people visiting, laughing and remembering Margaret. I had a DVD made with pictures of Margaret's life, and it played all afternoon as people stopped and remembered her. Flashes of Margaret as a child were mixed with shots of her with her family, of the flowers that she loved and of our pets. I included a list of things that she loved, everything from her favorite color, green, to her favorite food, canned sardines.

After people left, the family went out for pizza. Following dinner, everyone was tired and called it a night. I retired to our room, the room where Margaret and I had spent so many nights. I sat on the edge of the bed with a nightcap of sherry, trying to put the day into some sort of perspective. Failing that, I tried putting Margaret's death into a perspective that I could at least understand because accepting it was far off in the future. But that night, no wisdom came. Instead, there were tears and questions and doubts. I don't know how long I sat there, unable to make sense of much and unable to move.

Afterword: A Look Back With Love

"Life asks us to make measurable progress in reasonable time. That is why they make those 4th grade chairs so small." —*Jim Rohn*

As I write this, it has been almost three years since I lost Margaret, and in some ways, it still seems fresh. At the same time, change has been an important part of the healing process.

Until you have gone through the kind of loss that breaks your heart and tries to break your spirit, you can't know what gets you through it. And what helped me may not be the right answer for you, but I came out on the other side. If somebody had asked me that day in the garden when all I knew was that Margaret and her flowers were gone, if I would ever be OK, I couldn't have given an answer.

It began way before I was even vaguely aware of it. I had to try and write Margaret's obituary. The day after she died I spent much of the day sitting and attempting to put into words her amazing life, and at the end of the day I had failed terribly. I kept thinking that I couldn't do it, and on that day I was right. But the next day all of a sudden it flowed. Dona, who is the author of two books, tuned it up for me and Helen, my office assistant, typed it up and took it to the newspapers.

I needed to do this work for myself. Not only did it keep me busy and keep me from focusing on my loss, but it made me feel like there were things I could get done. One of the difficult lessons I learned from watching Margaret battle cancer and trying to help, is that there are times when there isn't much you can honestly do to effect change, and blaming yourself for it is a dangerous thing.

Making arrangements for Margaret helped me get back into a frame of mind where what I was actually making things happen. That lesson came in handy when we looked at preparing her memorial which I felt I couldn't do. So we decided to put it off a month. Her son David couldn't believe it, "You are going to wait a month?"

But that is what made sense, which leads me to another lesson learned. People are always going to have their perspectives on how things should be done. Their viewpoints can be legitimate and make sense. But, in the end, the best thing that you can do is to listen patiently, consider it honestly, and follow your best instinct. Then be prepared to live with your decision.

I started to make preparations for the memorial, dealing with the church, renting what we needed for the reception and planning how things would work. The will and trusts, the legal end of things, had mostly all been taken care of so that wasn't a concern for us.

I started working longer hours at the office. While Margaret was sick, I was working someplace between 20 and 30 hours a week, but now I was up to 40 hours a week. It was good because I was in a place where I was busy and comfortable. Again, my focus was on moving ahead.

I don't think it is healthy to sit in a dark room by yourself alone with a heavy heart. You need to get out, stay busy, push yourself just a little past what feels comfortable.

The thing that is true while you cared for your loved one is still true after they are gone, life keeps rolling along. And while people are even more willing to cut you slack and sympathize with your loss, the world keeps spinning. You have to be in it.

One of the things that happens when you are a caregiver is you become less socially engaged because you have to. But it's important to begin talking with people, putting yourself into situations where you will move beyond your loss a little.

You may also be surprised at the number of people who will reach out to you. People have a wonderful capacity for kindness and they want to help. If I was to offer a word of advice it would be to let them.

This doesn't mean you should push your feelings of loss off, or that moving on in any way should lessen the memory of your loved one, indeed it won't. It has been almost three years since Margaret died and she is still missed and I still think of her often.

I guess what I am saying is that if you make the effort to stay busy and be in touch, you will find things beginning to seem lighter. In the days and the weeks following Margaret's death I honestly didn't know what I could do and I thought my life was destined to be pretty difficult.

But I worked hard, put myself out there a bit and gradually things seemed to get better. I started going to functions, getting back into things that had been important to me before Margaret got sick. I started attending water district meetings, keeping track of the wet stuff again. I knew people at these meetings and I certainly knew water, so there was some comfort there.

A number of months after I first started going to the meetings, I had dinner with a woman who regularly attended the meetings, thinking the companionship was nice. From that friendship, over time, a romance grew.

Today, we are happily married. I have no regrets and I'm not ashamed that I found someone after I lost Margaret, though there are members of the family who do not understand our happiness.

And just because I have found love with another person, doesn't mean that I stopped loving Margaret or that our life together loses something. To be honest, if I hadn't been so happy with Margaret, I don't think there is any way that I could have become involved with anyone else.

A friend of mine tells me that a man who has a successful marriage and becomes widowed is more likely to remarry sooner rather than later, and I guess I believe that.

Losing Margaret was the hardest thing I have ever gone through emotionally, when I was in the middle of it, trying my best to take care of her on the outside and struggling mightily on the inside, I didn't know how I was going to get through it. Now as I look back, I realize that it's a long process and maybe the most important thing you can do is put one foot in front of the other, moving forward one day at a time.

I don't think that means you move away from your loved one. Rather, it means that your life keeps going and you take their love and that experience with you.

Acknowledgements

There are many people I would like to acknowledge for the success of *Three Months: A Caregiving Journey from Heartbreak to Healing*. First and foremost, Margaret's family, especially her daughter Dona, who helped me take care of Margaret. I am also indebted to my family, especially my three daughters, Christina, Jody and Erica whose support pushed and shoved me into sharing this tale of life and death.

I also want to mention Bill Meagher, a writer and good friend who provided guidance as well as literary ability and style to help bring this book to life. Of course I am also grateful to all my proofreaders here at my engineering firm and my administrative assistant and friend, Helen Coale who typed up my rambling notes into chapters. I believe she did as much crying as I did.

Special mention must also be made of Sandra Friedemann, another administrative assistant and book author, who continuously corrected both grammar and the book's structure, and Gerry Palter, our Human Resources person who helped with copy editing and Emma Wnuk, whose feedback about the book's humanity was essential.

Finally, I want to recognize all the caregivers, doctors and cancer survivors in this world who have experienced many of the same issues that are addressed in *Three Months: A Caregiving Journey from Heartbreak to Healing*. They are the silent heroes of this book.

Index

J. Dietrich Stroeh

J. Dietrich Stroeh an expert on water issues and a founding partner of CSW/Stuber Stroeh Engineering Group, spent 20 years with the Marin Municipal Water District, the last 6 years as the General Manager who solved the 25-month Marin drought of 1976-77. Diet is married with five children and seven grandchildren. He lives in Novato, California.

Duncan Garrett Photography

Bill Meagher

Bill Meagher's work has appeared in newspapers and magazines throughout California as well as on PBS and CBS. He covers commercial real estate and alternative investment on a national basis for Dealflow Media. He is a contributing editor for NorthBay biz Magazine and writes a monthly column called Only in Marin. Three Months is his first book, though he is currently wrapping up his first novel. When he is not writing he spends time with his wife Cindy and their cat Miles. He is a lifelong Giants fan and could not be happier with their 2010 World Series victory.

For more information and to contact the author, visit
www.threemonthsbook.com

CPSIA information can be obtained at www.ICGtesting.com
Printed in the USA
LVOW071837170212

269114LV00002B/1/P